MW00464490

The Mystery of

Harry Potter

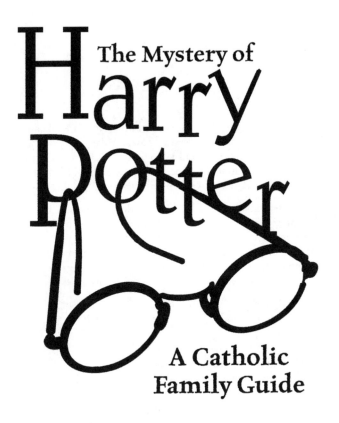

The Mystery of
Harry Potter

A Catholic Family Guide

Nancy Carpentier Brown

Our Sunday Visitor Publishing Division
Our Sunday Visitor, Inc.
Huntington, Indiana 46750

Copyright © 2007 by Our Sunday Visitor Publishing Division
Our Sunday Visitor, Inc. Published 2007

12 11 10 09 08 07   1 2 3 4 5 6 7 8 9

Our Sunday Visitor Publishing Division
Our Sunday Visitor, Inc.
200 Noll Plaza
Huntington, IN 46750

ISBN 978-1-59276-398-6 (Inventory No. T497)
LCCN: 2007929144

Cover design by Lindsey Luken
Interior design by Sherri L. Hoffman

Cover graphics courtesy of Shutterstock
Chesterton glasses courtesy of Ted Schluenderfritz Illustration and Design (5sparrows.com)

PRINTED IN THE UNITED STATES OF AMERICA

To Michael, Sarah, and Robin, with love.
You three are my team, my support group,
and my family. You're the best.

To all my blog friends —
who read and comment on Flying Stars,
www.mrsnancybrown.blogspot.com —
for your encouragement, feedback,
love, and prayers —
thanks.

Contents

Chapter One

The Mystery of Harry Potter

Why I Didn't Want to Read Harry Potter in the First Place

Have you read the Harry Potter books yet? Maybe your children read them, or want to, but you feel uncertain as to whether you should let them or not. Or, you've heard about them and need a guide to help you decide if your family should read them. You're wondering if you can give them to your children without guilt.

Some of you have not read the books, so my plan is to give away as little of the plot as possible, while still letting you know certain things so you can decide whether the books should be read in your family. The books are mysteries, and I don't want to spoil them for you.

Here are the book titles and reference letters.

Book One — *Harry Potter and the Sorcerer's Stone* (SS)
Book Two — *Harry Potter and the Chamber of Secrets* (CS)
Book Three — *Harry Potter and the Prisoner of Azkaban* (PA)
Book Four — *Harry Potter and the Goblet of Fire* (GF)
Book Five — *Harry Potter and the Order of the Phoenix* (OP)
Book Six — *Harry Potter and the Half-Blood Prince* (HBP)
Book Seven — *Harry Potter and the Deathly Hallows* (DH)

Harry Potter gets constant media attention. The books, the movies, the actors, the video games; every time there's

something new, it's news. A mother in Georgia fights to keep Potter out of her daughter's school — it's news.

Quite often Christian Fundamentalists oppose the series because they don't want their children exposed to witchcraft. Parents concerned about Wicca believe the books attract children to the occult. A priest who sees a blurred line between good and evil, or who's heard Harry breaks the rules to save the day, and doesn't believe it teaches children good morals, warns parents to keep away.

The author of the Harry Potter series, Joanne Kathleen (J.K.) Rowling has managed to tell a moral story in a magical story. Many of the Potter foes have not read the books. Some have read them as a fact-finding trip to gain evidence for their literalist beliefs.

There are Catholics who don't oppose Harry Potter. But of those who do, they consider the books an introduction to witchcraft and wizardry, showing such things in a positive light, and introducing children to a world better left alone. An occasional few dislike the books because of what they perceive to be poor writing.

Joseph Cardinal Ratzinger once wrote a private letter about the Potter books. In it, he told an author who wondered if Harry Potter was good or evil that such books had a "subtle seduction." This was a personal statement to one woman and not an *ex cathedra* pronouncement.

There is also a vocal church exorcist who at least twice has indicated that the Potter books portray witchcraft and are evil.

Based on these things, a self-respecting faithful Catholic parent might be inclined to think the books should be banned from the family and school bookshelves.

That's what I thought, until a friend convinced me to read the books and I had an experience that changed my outlook on the Harry Potter series.

Wait a minute. Why would I *even read* the books after all I know about them? Let me describe what happened.

My Trusted Catholic Friend Shocks Me

When the Harry Potter phenomenon first began, I was skeptical of it. I shy away from the popular culture: we don't own a TV; we homeschool our children; we monitor what books they read and what movies they watch. I heard rumblings about witchcraft and paganism, so the Harry Potter books were a distant blip on our family radar screen. There is plenty of other fiction to choose from.

Then, our daughter asked if she could read the books. I explained to her why I thought they might be bad. We discussed the books on and off, but I didn't let her read them.

A friend and I were talking on the phone one day. I considered her to be a good Catholic mother, a homeschooler like myself, so I was utterly shocked when she confessed that she'd not only read the Harry Potter books, but had allowed her teen children to read them too. She said she liked them, she said they were good. My first reaction was to think *Now I can't let my children play with her children.* After the shock wore off, I hesitated. *Wait a minute*, I said to myself. *Either my friend — whom I've always trusted — is way off base, or the Harry Potter books aren't what I've believed they are.* I decided it was time to find out for myself.

I read the book, *Harry Potter and the Sorcerer's Stone*, to my eleven-year-old daughter. The first book told an interesting story, but had scary elements. It wasn't witchcraft, which I hadn't noticed as I read the book, that bothered me so much as the life-and-death battle near the end of the story. Even though Harry Potter was eleven years old in the first book, most eleven-year-olds aren't faced with life and death battles. I thought the book was a little advanced for a child this age and was glad I hadn't given in and started reading it to my daughter at a younger age — or worse, let her read it by herself. By the end of the first book someone is dead and the scary words of the evil villain echo memorably. It was intense for a sheltered home-educated child, but by reading

it together, we discussed the scenes and decided the book was good.

We started *Harry Potter and the Chamber of Secrets*. This book had even scarier elements in it, beginning with non-fatal attacks on school children and ending with another life and death struggle between good and evil. My daughter and I talked over these incidents, and I could tell she was managing them fine; even though I had again been concerned the books were too intense. We started to read *Harry Potter and the Prisoner of Azkaban*. The book began much as the first two did, except it was a lot thicker, and I didn't have the wherewithal to read another one out loud. Harry had a rest in our house.

I didn't give the books much thought. The story line was compelling, Harry Potter was someone you cared about and identified with; the mysteries were interesting, and the plots complex enough to hold the reader's (even an adult's) interest. There was no danger of witchcraft entering our house from these books, the magic is used as any fantasy or fictional work might use magic, as a literary device, just as "faster than light speed" and "let's make the jump into hyper-space" and "transporters" are used in science fiction. Everyone knows these things aren't real; it's part of the story's setting.

We read the Edward Eager series in our house, the E. Nesbit titles, *Mary Poppins*, *The Hobbit*, *Narnia*, and many other books, which use magic as a literary device as well. Harry Potter isn't *about* magic. Harry Potter is about people: who we are, what we're on earth for, why we do good and fight evil, and how we make choices. There was no mention of God or Satan as the power behind anything — the books aren't religious. The line between good and evil was defined. Harry is on the side of good, and although he isn't a perfect character, he's human and the reader identifies with him.

At this point I was no longer anti-Harry — though I wasn't quite pro-Harry. I simply felt the books were not a danger to my child. Otherwise, I felt neutral about them.

I thought no one should protest against them, neither should anyone go out of their way to recommend them.

As for the future Pope, I respect his opinion, but doubted that he had actually read any of the Harry Potter books. I felt he made his comments as a polite response to a lady who sent him her book. He was responding privately to her, not publicly placing the Potter series on the Banned Books list, as some people interpreted his remarks. (For more on this situation, please read Regina Doman's article "Harry Potter for Catholics?" which can be found at www.zossima.com/harryforcatholics.htm.)

Before long, our second child began asking to read the Potter series. I made her wait; but the moment she turned eleven, *Harry Potter and the Sorcerer's Stone* came home with us from the library, and I was about to return to the world of Hogwarts School. I proceeded in the same way, reading SS and CS out loud, and then I let her read the next books on her own. My older daughter re-read the books at this time.

Left Out of the Discussion

Then my two girls began discussing Harry Potter. They talked about it in the car. They talked about it at the supper table. They talked about it in their bedrooms, sharing their thoughts and feelings about the story line, the characters, and what they thought was going to happen next in the series.

They talked about characters I didn't know and hadn't heard of. Who was Sirius Black? And Mad-Eye Moody? What in the world was a Quidditch World Cup?

I began to feel left out. I wanted to share in my daughters' interesting conversations, but I couldn't. I wanted to answer their questions but I hadn't read the other four books. I admit I didn't know if the next four followed the same pattern as the first two. I questioned if I should let my

---

Read Them Yourself

You don't have time. You're working, changing diapers, and making decorations for the next 2nd grade room party. You've got carpooling and shopping to worry about, and the next mortgage payment. Read an 800-page children's book? I must be joking, right? No, I'm not. You have time. Just start reading the first one. I think you'll see what I mean. Next thing you know, you'll be keeping that book in the bathroom, or in the kitchen next to the stove, and you'll be reading it while you stir the spaghetti. Trust me. You *have* time to read them. Now get going. You need to go get a book at the library, don't you? (Pssst — that's Rowling, in Children's Fiction under "R" — you want the first book, *Harry Potter and the Sorcerer's Stone.*)

---

girls read the books on their own. I knew my 14-year-old had good sense but what if there was something in there she didn't *know* was bad?

I Had to Read the Books for Myself

I did what any self-respecting mother would do under similar circumstances. I took *Harry Potter and the Prisoner of Azkaban* out of the library and started getting caught up. My children were amused to see I was interested in their books.

After I read PA, I went on to GF and OP. Something happened when I got to Book Five, *Harry Potter and the Order of the Phoenix.*

As I read the first four books, I cruised along on the surface, enjoying the books for the adventure and mystery. I found myself interested in the characters, and particularly in Harry. I was rooting for him, wanting him to succeed, feeling bad for his mistakes and failures to act, noticing a lot of human qualities in him I had myself: a desire to do right,

wanting to fight evil, but a tendency to get angry and emotional.

Something Deep

While reading OP I noticed something: a deeper level of meaning. Reacting to the book, I wrote this on my blog:

Life is a battle. A constant struggle. A war. Mostly within ourselves.

One thing this Harry Potter Summer Reading thing has done for me is to help me think about the daily battle. J.K. Rowling visualizes the battle, and shows us a real enemy. I am reminded of our real life battle with Satan, sin, and temptation, and I need a plan of action, a battle plan. I must practice my own Defense Against the Dark Arts.

— Flying Stars, 8/18/06,
www.mrsnancybrown.blogspot.com

That week, I practiced fighting the sin in my life, and practiced working on the virtues. Thinking about what I was doing as "practicing" made it easier. I didn't think of myself as succeeding or failing. I thought of the work I was doing on my spiritual life as *practicing*, and for the first time in ages, I felt able to say no to ever-present temptations. I felt the saints were on my side helping me, and I felt good about what I was doing. And I had to credit the Harry Potter books.

What spiritual struggle challenges you? What one thing could you "practice" working on? Laziness? Overeating? Overindulging? Watching too much TV? Surfing the Internet longer than you need to? Lack of generosity? Selfishness?

I began to think about the spiritual aspects of the Potter books, and consulting with other Catholics, I realized there was another level of understanding the books, a spiritual level. I could see where someone could read the series and never find that deeper level. The books could be read as mysteries and adventures and enjoyed. Or read as witchcraft and magic and rejected.

But even at the surface, most people reading the books sense good overcoming evil, of evil being unattractive and deadly, and fighting the good fight.

The books are set in another world, a world of witches and wizards, casting spells, mixing potions, doing hexes and charms, and talking about magic as if there were a good side and a dark side. But since magic is used in the story like a talent, the reader understands that the use of our talents can either be for good or ill, too.

There is a so-called religion recognized by the government and the military and even some hospitals called Wicca, in which people who claim to be witches and warlocks do practice witchcraft and spells, dabbling in the dark arts.

The fact Wicca exists and is attracting followers, including our vulnerable young people, makes a book that portrays witches in a positive light scary. *If* Harry Potter was about witchcraft and wizardry and Wicca.

Sister Teresa Maria, my second grade teacher. . . took care of an old woman on the fourth floor who was quite sick. . . intrigued. . . I climbed up the fire escape one day to see what it was all about. Looking directly at me through the window was the wicked witch from Snow White and the Seven Dwarfs, which I had recently seen. I jumped off the milk box. . . hurried up the street and entered the church. In my fear I rushed up to the altar of the Blessed Virgin. . . I knelt down to pray because I had

seen a witch. As I was praying, a question came into my mind: "How come the witch did not harm Sister Teresa?" The answer was obvious: Because she was good to the witch. I said to myself, "Maybe if people were nicer to witches, they wouldn't be quite so bad."

— Father Benedict Groeschel, C.F.R,
The Virtue Driven Life, pp. 141-142

The Supernatural World

The strongest argument to be made in defense of the "other world" setting of Harry Potter is our Catholic faith.

As believers, we too believe in another world. A world which exists here in our universe, a world where we can know about things others don't, a world in which we can link to people "beyond the veil," a world right alongside the natural world, called the supernatural world.

We believe that, as Harry was marked with a sign on his forehead in his infancy, we too are marked with a sign of faith at our infant baptism on our foreheads; a sign this world can't understand, and can't imagine makes a difference. We believe Love leaves a permanent mark. We believe the highest form of love is to "give up one's life for another."

We believe, just as Harry goes to school and learns about his world, our children do not learn the faith by osmosis, but must be taught the Ten Commandments, the Beatitudes, the *Catechism*, and the meaning of the Scriptures and sacraments, either by a parent or teacher. Our children learn morals through stories, real stories, as in the Bible, and fairy tales, like "Jack and the Beanstalk" or Harry Potter.

We believe, like Harry, that a circle of friends around makes us stronger on life's journey. Harry has traveled with Hermione and Ron (his two best friends in the series) throughout his school career, and we travel with family, friends, pastors, and teachers.

We believe, like Harry, there is a battle going on, and as he forms Dumbledore's Army (Professor Albus Dumbledore is the head of the good guys in the Potter stories), we belong to the Church Militant, fighting in this world for right, truth, freedom, and goodness.

J.K. Rowling has created (or sub-created) an overlapping secondary universe. She shows children and adults the possibility of another world. Some of the non-magical people (called Muggles in the Rowling stories) see things happening in their world, but choose to ignore whatever it is, as it doesn't fit with the things they understand. Skeptics in our own world "see" things too: miracles, prayers answered, people attending church on a regular basis, the faithful relying on God for help; it doesn't fit in with what they want to understand, and they ignore the evidence, often explaining events as the result of an overactive imagination.

On the other hand, there is a case to be made for the use of caution with Harry Potter.

Harry Potter is for mature audiences. Parental guidance is necessary. As the series progresses, the themes increase in maturity. A child of eight may be ready for SS and CS, but not be ready for the violence in PA and the death in GF; and won't be ready for the teenage relationship issues in OP and HBP. The books have frightening and intense scenes in them

---

The Two Worlds

Harry Potter — The Muggle or non-magical world; and the Wizarding world, full of dragons, and wise wizards, a school to train its wizarding young, and a government, the Ministry of Magic, to oversee its people.

Humanity — The human world, or the natural world, which we can see, hear, taste and touch; and the supernatural world, an unseen world of a Trinitarian God, his mother, the saints, angels, and devils.

— which children *can* handle if they are ready and have a parent guide.

Some say that the Harry Potter books are fine for all children. They give children an evil enemy to be frightened of, but they also provide readers with a "St. George" to slay the dragons. There *are* children who are going to be fine reading them 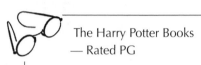 on their own. The problem is there are also sensitive children out there — and I have one myself so I know — who are not going to be okay with these when they are too young to handle it — even though they may be begging us to read the books to them and feel certain that they can handle it. You know your sensitive child best. These are the children who already have a hard time falling asleep at night because they fear the normal things: the dark, the unknown of sleep, what's in the closet or under the bed, and those scary shadows on the wall. Add the imagery of the books, and you might now have a child who needs a high degree of parental involvement in order to go to bed. Every parent gets to choose. I decided that for my sensitive person, the Harry Potter books had to wait until she turned eleven, when I determined she was more able to remember that evil can be defeated, and not dwell overly on the evil itself.

The books are excellent reading for adults. Adults find word play and humor, love the twisted and complex plots, keep track of running bits and plot line clues and red herrings, and enjoy the literary references. The books are good for children with parental guidance — if you decide they are for your children. The central theme of the books is the victory of Love over Death, which is a mature theme.

When the series is read together, the books prompt discussions. Harry Potter could be the source of dinner conversation for months. The books can be an opportunity for

> The Harry Potter Books
> — Rated PG

Dinner Table Questions

Why is Dumbledore good?

Why is Voldemort bad?

How did Harry get his scar?

Does Harry miss his parents? What did they do before they died?

Which people act as Harry's parents in the story?

Why is Draco interested in pure-bloods? What does Hagrid say about it?

What is Harry good at? What is Harry not so good at?

Why is Snape so mean? Is he evil or good?

Catholic parents to discuss important life issues with their children.

If the reader is looking for a blanket statement giving permission to give Harry Potter to your children because I say they are safe, you will not find that here. I do not recommend just giving the books to your children. I recommend reading them together, and using them as a springboard for many interesting discussions.

What About the Author?

Belloc is one of my favourite poets for his wit, his understatement, and his profundity — but, perhaps most of all, for the lion called Ponto who ate Jim.

— J.K. Rowling in *Once Upon A Poem*

After discovering Harry Potter, I tried to find out all that I could about the author of the books, J.K. Rowling. Although she's a bit shy and reclusive, there are biographies and web sites with information about her.

She reads C.S. Lewis, Jane Austen, J.R.R. Tolkien, and E. Nesbit; a favorite poem of Hilaire Belloc's hangs framed on her study wall; her favorite painting is a Caravaggio called "The Supper at Emmaus"; she belongs to the UK Chesterton Society; she quotes Dorothy Sayers and Charles Dickens; her favorite music is Beethoven's *Appassionata* Piano Sonata, although she listened to a Tchaikovsky violin concerto almost daily during her first pregnancy; she attends the (Presbyterian) Church of Scotland and has had her three children baptized; finding out these details about Rowling served to increase my interest in her books.

G.K. Chesterton and the Battle of Lepanto

"Lepanto" is one of G.K. Chesterton's best poems. For those unfamiliar with Chesterton, he was a prolific journalist of the 20th century.

> *He said something about everything and he said it better than anybody else. But he was no mere wordsmith. He was very good at expressing himself, but more importantly, he had something very good to express. The reason he was the greatest writer of the 20th century was because he was also the greatest thinker of the 20th century.*
>
> — Dale Ahlquist on Chesterton

Why am I bringing up a Chesterton poem in a book about Harry Potter? Because the story lines are quite similar, and no one debates Chesterton's honored place on the Catholic family bookshelf.

Chesterton's poem "Lepanto" tells about a battle between good and evil on both the physical and spiritual plane. The battle itself, a sea attack, pitted the navy of Turkish forces, led by Ali Pasha, bent on invading Europe, threat-

ening to attack both Venice and Rome, which could have brought about the collapse of Christian Europe; against the Christian navy, led by a youthful unknown. (Chesterton, *Lepanto, with Notes and Commentary*, 1.)

Like Harry and his friends fighting against the evil Lord Voldemort, the odds were against the Christians in the battle of Lepanto. In the same way the Ministry of Magic won't help Harry and Dumbledore, the Holy League would get no help from Germany, divided and weakened by the Protestant Reformation, or any of the other European monarchs. A youthful boy, Don John of Austria, like Harry, takes charge and leads the Christians to victory.

The Battle of Lepanto, like the battle going on in the Harry Potter series, is taking place on the spiritual level. Preserving Christian Europe is good. Defending land belonging to you and which is under attack is a just cause. Will the Christians succeed in keeping the invaders from taking over the land by force? The powerful head of the Turks, the sultan, Selim II, like Voldemort, wants more power, more land, more slaves. Selim's desire for power leads him to believe, like Voldemort, he can take what isn't his.

I'll use the poetry of "Lepanto" throughout this book to demonstrate how the spiritual warfare of Harry Potter is like the sea battle of 1571, when the Turkish forces commanded by Selim's admiral, Ali Pasha, met up with the Christian forces led by Don John of Austria.

⋆ Questions to Ponder

1. What have you heard about the Harry Potter books? Did you question whether the series is good or bad for your family?
2. What are your views of the Harry Potter series?
3. Have your friends read the books? What do they think?
4. Are the author's beliefs important when deciding on what books to read? Why or why not?

Up Next

Now, let us find out together who should read Harry Potter, if the Potter stories are "too dark," and whether or not the stories promote witchcraft, sorcery, New Age thinking, or make the occult look attractive to young people.

Chapter Two

Is Harry Potter the Kind of Literature We Should Read?

Who Should Read Harry Potter?

I cringe when I hear Harry Potter read by teachers to children in second grade. Or that Harry Potter is required reading for a fifth grade class. Although there are children in the classroom ready to hear the stories, not *every* child is. The first book is less intense than those following, each book grows more intense, and therefore, the appropriate age for each book goes up, depending on the individual child's maturity.

I dislike classroom reading of the books because the stories should be discussed within the family, by parents who know their faith. A teacher might be restricted from explaining that the phoenix represents resurrection. The Headmaster Dumbledore has a pet phoenix throughout the series names Fawkes. Fawkes rescues Harry in one book, sings a funeral song in another, and plays an important role in the books.

The phoenix has traditionally been viewed as a symbol of Easter — the resurrection — because it is a mythical bird that dies periodically by burning itself up, and then rises again from its ashes. There are phoenix stained glass windows in some Catholic Churches. The Church Fathers used the phoenix to communicate the mystery of the resurrection of the flesh and the concepts of virginity, chastity and filial piety. The public school teacher might be afraid to connect Transfiguration classes with the Transfiguration of Christ in her classroom. The teacher might not be at liberty to discuss good and evil.

Harry Potter Book	Appropriate Ages (depending on the child and maturity level)
Sorcerer's Stone	7-11 to adult
Chamber of Secrets	8-11 to adult
Prisoner of Azkaban	9-11 to adult
Goblet of Fire	10-12 to adult
Order of the Phoenix	10-13 to adult
Half-Blood Prince	11-14 to adult
Deathly Hallows	12-14 to adult

It frustrates me to read about movie merchandise targeted to four to nine-year olds, who are much too young for a movie rated PG-13. I know one mom who let her son read the books, but when the Goblet of Fire movie came out rated PG-13, she previewed it and thought it was too violent. Because Harry is going through adolescence, more mature themes are introduced with each successive school year. Harry develops a crush, and Ron acts immaturely toward a female student out of jealousy. Eight-year olds do not need to be exposed to these issues.

I believe parents should read the books first. This is a good idea for a great many books, not just Harry Potter. Even the Bible can be confusing without parents. For example, Jesus says to become like little children to enter the Kingdom of Heaven. And St. Paul says that when he was a child, he thought like a child, but then he put aside childish things. Which way should we follow? In the same way, in the Old Testament God instructs the Israelites to wipe out an entire people; and yet Jesus, in the New Testament, tells us to love our enemies, and do good to those who would do us harm.

After reading the Potter stories for themselves, parents have a good idea if their child can handle the intensity of

the storyline. Read the book aloud to a child who is mature enough. Another choice is listening to an audio recording together. Least desirable is letting your child read it without knowing what's in it yourself, thinking you are off the hook because someone says the books are okay: I rate the books PG, in need of parental guidance. Your children *need* your guidance with the series. This book strives to provide you with guidance so together you and your family can share the Potter books, using them as an opportunity to start interesting conversations together.

Also undesirable is allowing children to see the movies without reading the books. If you've already done this, it might be time to take a trip to the library and check out the books. You'll be able to discuss what was left out of the movies, how the movies differ from the books and if it makes any difference to how the story works out. You can talk about how much better the books are than the movies.

The magic and the witchcraft should be addressed, which is easy to do. If a parent said, "You know, honey, J.K. Rowling doesn't believe in magic, dragons and spells herself. She's just pretending about the magic, using her imagination to tell a story, like a fairy tale," it's enough. Even if you don't have time to read the books with your children, you can say this. If you've grounded your children in their faith, they'll read the book through with the eyes of their beliefs — the beliefs you've instilled in them.

The movies are not the books. Preview the movies before allowing your children to watch them — they are scary for many young people. Pay attention to the ratings. Movies One, Two, and Three are rated PG, Four is rated PG-13, yet Decent Films rates all four movies "Teen & Up" for good reasons. Check on line to see why they have the ratings they do (www.decentfilms.com) at Decent Films.

Not Just Should You: Why Should You?

Beyond the point of whether anyone reads Harry Potter, is the deeper question of *why* should anyone read Harry Potter?

We could ask ourselves, why read novels at all? Why read fiction? Isn't it all escapism, and a waste of time for a true Christian? Years ago, I gave up novels for Lent, which extended into many years. I thought they were a waste of time. G.K. Chesterton's work brought me back to novel reading. There are *good* stories out there. Stories can improve our lives.

> When people found out I was writing a Catholic book about Harry Potter, their first question was always, "Are you FOR or AGAINST Harry?" and I say: "I'm **for** parents deciding for themselves what's right for their own family."

For example, sometimes, when we read about a hero persevering through a particularly troublesome situation, we suddenly think of our own lives and how if we were just 1/10th as persistent as the fictional hero, we could manage to get through our own hard times. When I read *David Copperfield*, by Charles Dickens, I remember thinking, *My childhood was easy street compared to David's. I should never complain again.* In the same way, it was while reading *The Man Who Was Thursday* by G. K. Chesterton, that I thought about how children rebel against their parents, and that I should take care not to be too strict nor too lenient with my children.

What good can the Harry Potter books do for me as a Catholic? On the light side: the books provide amusement and relaxation. Our lives should be a healthy balance of work and play, activity and rest. While relaxing, one could, in addition to refreshing the body, refresh the soul with a good, select work of fiction. Harry Potter isn't spiritual reading, but it can aid the spiritual life, as it helps one think

about such things as love, death, honor, morality, steadfast-ness, friendship, kindness, temptations, etc. There are rich images in Harry Potter, teaching elements, and ideas which cause the reader to become meditative.

Do the Harry Potter Books Overemphasize Evil?

I guess you could ask, is evil a reality or not? If it isn't, then the books talk a lot about something that isn't real. If evil is real, as Catholics believe, then the books do nothing more than address that reality in a work of fiction.

Evil entered our world long before Harry Potter came along. Harry Potter does not bring more evil into the world, or show children, in any way that evil is to be desired. There are scenes where the Dark Lord Voldemort acts in character: he's evil. It's easy for parents to pause here and discuss this with their children, saying "since Voldemort is like Satan, and Satan is the Father of Lies, if he said there is no good and evil we know that it's a lie, right?" and "Harry was right to call Voldemort a liar, wasn't he?" and move on with the story.

Are the Harry Potter Books Too Dark?

The stories are dark because they are dealing with life and death, good and evil. Jesus dying on the cross is very dark, too, but we know the rest of the story. How can we tell the story of the Resurrection if we don't first tell the story of the Crucifixion?

The stag is a traditional symbol for Christ. Harry Potter's father was what Rowling calls an "animagus," or a person who can transform temporarily into an animal. Each person's animal form reveals a characteristic of that person. For example, the betrayer in the story turns into a rat. The gentle godfather can turn into a big friendly dog. Harry Potter's father could turn into a majestic stag. The stag is

also featured in the stained glass work in many churches. The deer represents Jesus Christ, who kills the serpent or dragon. The stag kills, which sounds evil, but it must kill the serpent in self-defense.

I'm not saying there is no danger in the Harry Potter books. There can be a danger in the hands of people who either read the books the wrong way, or don't discuss them with their children. It can also be a danger when children have questions answered by other children, the Internet, or a teacher who can't talk about religion in school. I believe if the books are read with the eyes of faith, and shared by Catholic parents with their children, good can come out of it. The family's faith can be strengthened and many good conversations will flow from the ideas in these novels.

No one *has* to read Harry Potter. Anyone who wishes to, can avoid the whole series, for there are plenty of other great books out there for our children to read.

Literature *is* important in the life of a Catholic. We are all influenced by stories. Sometimes stories teach us more about morality than straight lectures from our parents, or straight sermons from the pulpit. That's why young children are often read fairy tales, which have a moral to the

More Dinner Table Questions

In the book of Revelation, Chapter Four verse six, St. John describes the four living creatures: a lion, a calf, an animal with a face like a man, and an eagle. The early Church fathers applied this vision to the four gospel writers. John is often depicted as an eagle, Matthew as the man, Luke as the calf or ox, and Mark as the Lion. These gospel writers are often portrayed in Church architecture or decoration as these four creatures. Look up the reasons for each saint's depiction in a Catholic encyclopedia or on the Internet. What animal would represent you? Why?

story. Stories can have a powerful effect on us and on the world; they can transform our world from a namby-pamby wishy-washy "we are now beyond good and evil" mentality, to a true "right vs. wrong" and "good vs. evil" mentality. Christianity produces great writers and J.K. Rowling is a Christian writer. Her books use a clever literary device: witchcraft, which attracts millions of readers who absorb a subtle education in Christian morality.

What is J.K Rowling's motivation? Is it greed? Biographies indicate that she was inspired one day while on a train ride and thought up a story about a boy named Harry Potter. She was a teacher and a part-time secretary, who wrote stories at her typewriter during lunch breaks. When she thought up Harry Potter, she had no idea whether the story would sell. In fact, the book was rejected by at least 12 different publishing houses. Rowling is a writer who reads, and she wrote a story she felt compelled to write — a story she would love to read herself, she said. Her success, in many ways, is a complete mystery. Why do readers love Harry Potter? Because he's a wizard? No. Rather, because he's a down and out boy, an orphan whom we sympathize with, an outcast who needs love, and acts bravely when faced with difficult circumstances.

Several of Harry Potter's critics have had dealings with the occult or New Age type practices. They are looking through the lens of their past experiences. A child raised in a Catholic home who has not had such affiliations will not focus on the occult. If your children have had ties with Wicca or Satanism, you need to use extra caution in reading the books, or any fantasy novel that deals with magic, even such classics as *The Lord of the Rings*. In such a case, it's even more important to read the books together, if you choose to read them at all, looking for the Christian symbolism and talking about it.

I see the spells and charms as window dressings. When the children in C.S. Lewis's books walk through the

wardrobe into Narnia, readers know it's fantasy. When owls begin delivering letters to Harry no matter where he is, even flying in through the fireplace, the readers know it's fantasy.

Children know a story when they read one, and can tell the magic is part of the story, and not of their real lives. They may *play* magic, or *play* Harry Potter in their playtime life if they have such free time, just as children pretend to celebrate Mass or pretend they are mommy and daddy. Playing "Harry" doesn't mean they are getting into the occult.

Four Thousand Pages Later . . .

The Harry Potter books are not overtly Christian. If they were, they wouldn't be so popular. That's just a book publishing industry fact. Why *are* the books popular? Why do children and adults read these books by the millions? The Harry Potter books are the best selling books of all time. The New York Times was pressured into creating a best selling list category for children's books because authors of adult fiction were complaining — a fact which serves in muddying the issue of whether the Harry Potter series are children's books. At one point in time, four of the Potter books occupied space on the Best Seller list.

The Potter books resonate with people in our times. We aren't allowed in polite company to speak politically incorrectly — that is — to call one thing right and another wrong.

Someone might *start* reading Harry Potter because it's popular and everyone else is reading it, but they wouldn't *continue* unless they liked the books. After all, the total number of pages in the seven book series is over 4,000. You have to *want* to read that many pages.

Even though hidden deep within each of us we know good and evil are realities. The Harry Potter story paints a tale of good vs. evil, and everyone must choose sides.

I believe the books are popular too, because they are well-written, intricately plotted mysteries. They satisfy an inner longing. They leave the reader wanting the good to win. The reader is attracted to the goodness in the characters.

People long for truth. We search for meaning, and Harry Potter delivers. For a literary analysis of why the Potter books ring true, see John Granger's book, *Looking for God in Harry Potter*. Mr. Granger is classically trained in Latin and Greek literature, as well as certified as a Great Books teacher. His book describes J.K. Rowling's classical training — top of her class in French, German, and English, double first in French and Classical Languages. Granger does an excellent job of describing the mythological and literary aspects of Harry Potter.

I believe J.K Rowling has pulled off the biggest coup of our age. She's got millions of readers in the palm of her hand, reading each of her installments. She has handed the world the biggest Christian tale of our times, disguised in a story about witches and wizards. So cleverly disguised, most of the world doesn't even realize what it's reading.

The Watchful Dragons

Let's take a look at C.S. Lewis for a moment and his comments about the "watchful dragons." For Lewis, the watchful dragons were the world's gatekeepers, those who tout political correctness, multicultural inclusiveness, tolerance, and making sure everybody has good, healthy, and high self-esteem. These are the people who hesitate to tell children one thing is right and another wrong for fear of hurt feelings.

These gatekeepers try to keep Christian material out of the school systems, out of public places and out of children's

minds, because they don't want children *brainwashed* by zealous theists.

Lewis says the watchful dragons guard against anything smelling religious.

CHESTERTON

White founts falling in the courts of the sun,
And the Soldan of Byzantium is smiling as they run;
There is laughter like the fountains in that face of all
     men feared,
It stirs the forest darkness, the darkness of his beard...
     — G.K. Chesterton, Lepanto, lines 1-4

Something very painful was going on in Harry's mind. As Hagrid's story came to a close, he saw again the blinding flash of green light, more clearly than he had ever remembered it before — and he remembered something else, for the first time in his life: a high, cold, cruel laugh.
     — SS, p. 56

In the poem "Lepanto," the "White founts falling in the courts of the sun" are the fountains in the Sultan's palace. The Soldan of Byzantium is Selim II (1524-1574), the Sultan of Constantinople, seat of the Turkish Ottoman Empire. "Soldan" is another word for "Sultan." When an evil man laughs, instead of bringing joy, it brings a chill of fear.

Harry Potter faces the evil laughter in his nemesis, Lord Voldemort, the man who murdered his parents and tried but failed to murder Harry. The laughter of the villain is cold and cruel because it isn't the laughter of joy and gladness, but of death and destruction.

I saw how stories of this kind [fairy and fantasy tales] could steal past a certain inhibition which had paralyzed much of my own religion in childhood. Why did one find it so hard to feel as one was told one ought to feel about God or about the sufferings of Christ? I thought the chief reason was that one was told one ought to. An obligation to feel can freeze feelings. And reverence itself did harm. The whole subject was associated with lowered voices; almost as if it were something medical. But supposing that by casting all these things into an imaginary world, stripping them of their stained-glass and Sunday school associations, one could make them for the first time appear in their real potency? Could one not thus steal past those watchful dragons? I thought one could.

> — C.S. Lewis, in "Sometimes Fairy Stories May Say Best What's to be Said," from *Of Other Worlds: Essays & Stories*, p. 37

I believe J.K Rowling has created just such a story. Because of its witches and wizards, it steals past the watchful dragons of children's literature and filmmaking.

✦ Questions to Ponder

1. Do I have the information I need as a Catholic parent to decide whether my family should read Harry Potter?

2. Do I have time to read the stories to my children, or listen with them?

3. Do my children have any particular sensitivities that would make it hard for them to handle the Potter books right now?

4. How do I usually decide about what books my children can read?

Up Next

In the next chapter, we'll explore the Bible, the catechism, and a "Catholic" view of Harry Potter.

Is Harry Potter Catholic?

Harry and Catholics

Here's something interesting I've noticed about Harry Potter and Catholics. Many Catholics don't think much about Harry. Their children go to school, the classmates talk about Harry Potter books, and most parents assume since Jenny's mother lets Jenny read the books, and since Jenny's mother is careful about things, the Potter books must be okay.

In certain Catholic circles, some homeschooling groups and apostolate type groups, the rumors have gone around for years that Harry Potter is bad. In fact, whether or not you let your children read Harry Potter is a litmus test to judge how good or bad a Catholic or how orthodox you are, in some circles.

In these groups, someone has read about Harry in a Catholic magazine, newspaper, or on-line. A well-respected Catholic is interviewed and states Potter is full of evil, witchcraft, the occult; and not just that: Harry is a rule breaker who often lies and disregards authority — a poor example for our children to follow. The respected person states the magic in Potter is different from the magic in *Narnia* or *The Lord of the Rings*; and we good Catholics should avoid it by not allowing Harry Potter into our homes.

After all, the old-fashioned novelist generally gave his hero some human weaknesses and his villain some redeeming merits.

— G.K. Chesterton

Although Harry Potter is criticized as being less than a perfect character, I've never heard anyone complain about Voldemort being less than completely evil. Voldemort has been described as pure evil, but as Chesterton states above, Rowling has given her villain some redeeming merits. As one example, when he has the power to kill a defenseless hero at the end of the Goblet of Fire book, Voldemort gives the boy the chance to defend himself.

Narnia isn't transparent as a Christian allegory. I know a person who read the books yearly from the age of 14 on. It wasn't until she was 35 she realized the books could be viewed as a Christian allegory.

The same thing is true of *The Lord of the Rings*. Tolkien's books were criticized just as the Potter books are: Witch-craft. Sorcery. Magic. Evil. Then there's the whole Dungeons and Dragons tangent. This role-playing game based on *The Lord of the Rings* books could become addictive. It wasn't until recently we've considered both *Narnia* and *The Lord of the Rings* as exemplary *Christian* stories.

Parents who hear about the Potter books from trusted Catholics on radio and TV avoid the books, wish they weren't in the library, tell other parents to avoid the books, and even post warnings on-line. I know. I was one of those Catholic parents on the receiving end of such e-mails, and I, too, was against the series — though I had not read them myself.

Later on, Catholic parents whom I considered thought-ful and discerning said positive things about Harry Potter. Then I began to give the matter another look. Why would these parents say the Potter books were okay, and even admit they were reading them to their children, if the books were evil — as I believed?

I read the books and changed my mind about what they contained. I started talking about them on line, and a host of Catholics, whom I considered deep thinkers, joined in the conversation. Chestertonians — those who admire and read

the works of the great English writer, G.K. Chesterton; life-long Catholics, recent converts, and I, all adults — were sharing ideas about Harry Potter and the spiritual life. I discovered a world of Catholic underground Pro-Harry supporters.

Catholics Opposing Harry Potter

I realized the number of Catholics who opposed the books was small, and often because of misunderstanding the books. Because they are vocal about their opposition I want to give voice to the Catholics who read Rowling's books and see in them a moral tale and think Harry is a good role model for our children.

Catholics, it seems to me, tend to look for the good in things, knowing that if God created something, it at least started out good. Of course things can go bad, for we believe in the fall, original sin, and the devil himself. Yet, the defendant is innocent until proven guilty.

Some folks tend to take books literally, and are unable to make distinctions. For example, even though the characters in Rowling's books are described as witches and wizards, they are people with talents or skills that can be used for good or evil. The literalists see the word "witch", and can quote the Bible condemning witchcraft. I agree, witchcraft is to be condemned and it's evil. Despite the fact that the characters are called witches, the Potter books are not *about* witchcraft.

Literalists often use the Bible against Harry Potter. Everything the Catholic Church teaches today about magic and sorcery is true: we are against it and should avoid it. That's why I'd never give my children *Practical Paganism for Parents and Children* by Ashleen O'Gaea, *LuLu Goes to Witch School* by Jane O'Connor and Emily Arnold McCully (for grades one and two), *Little Witch Learns to Read* by Sylvie Wickstrom and Deborah Hautzig (ages four to eight), or *How to Turn Your Ex-Boyfriend into a Toad: And*

Other Spells for Love, Wealth, Beauty, and Revenge by Deborah Gray and Athena Starwoman.

The literalists unknowingly use the text of Harry Potter against themselves. They believe if magic occurs in the novel, the use of magic is being advocated. And that if a character in the novel tells a lie, lying is advocated. This can't be true, since even the Bible has stories about magicians, and others about people lying.

Harry Potter Peripherals

People bundle the Harry Potter books with the Harry Potter commercialism, which began with the movies not the books. The books themselves do not invite commercialism or materialism; in fact, Rowling has an anti-commercialism message in her books. See, for example, what happens to the souvenirs Harry and Ron purchase at the Quidditch World Cup.

No one has to give money to the Harry Potter industry. Our family has checked the books out of the library, and we don't own action figures or other spin-off products. I am not trying to help out the multi-billion dollar Harry Potter industry by writing this book. My goal is to help you see that these popular books can be used to great effect as conversation starters in your house. I am not encouraging you to spend money.

Can Your Children Get *Too* Into Harry Potter?

Children and adults can go overboard with Harry. As with all things, moderation is the key. Read the books together. Read other books, too. If Harry Potter is consuming your children, take a break. I believe Harry is a good thing, but I know children can go too far, and parents need to be watchful of this. Just as you limit the time your children spend on the computer, watching TV, or talking on the phone, you

---

Too Into Harry?

- Will only choose Harry Potter to read
- Talks non-stop about Harry
- Wants to buy Potter items
- On Harry Potter web sites too much
- Seeks friends who have read Harry
- Can't get Harry out of his/her mind
- Discipline problems related to Harry Potter books

If your child has one or more of these symptoms, it's probably time for a break from Harry Potter.

---

can limit your children's exposure to Harry Potter. Even though Harry Potter is in the form of books and most parents are thrilled when their children are reading a book instead of playing a video game, children can become obsessed with books, too, so monitor your children.

Adults can get fanatical about Harry too. There may be even more temptations for parents, as the internet has many message boards and web sites where Harry Potter can be discussed, reviewed, and speculated upon, wasting time and energy better spent on family matters.

Leaky Lounge — Harry Potter discussion forum for movies, books, and more! www.leakynews.com
Registered Users: 51,640
Total Posts: 993,599

Harry = Occult?

Some vocal Christians seem insistent upon letting the world know Harry Potter is a subtle and ingeniously packaged introduction, attracting and luring children into the world of witchcraft and the occult. It doesn't make any difference

whether author J.K. Rowling has stated repeatedly in interviews that she does not believe in magic or witchcraft; she
is a Christian and attends the Church of Scotland, a Presbyterian church.

Even the old Dungeons and Dragons game, which was
developed after *The Lord of the Rings* book, got kids going
"too far" into that world. Despite J.R.R. Tolkien's Catholicism, the story could still be misconstrued and used for ill
instead of good. There is every possibility the Harry Potter
books can be misconstrued and used for ill; human beings
are prone to error, and can use good things for ill purposes.
To say the intent of the author is to lead children into the
occult is making assumptions that aren't there.

Could the books make witchcraft attractive without the
author intending it? Rowling has packaged a Christian story
with a wrapping of witchcraft and magic attractive to most
children today, and through this disguise has encouraged
millions of children to read a redemptive, moral story that
can perhaps teach more than a religion class ever could.
Jesus told parables for a reason. Rowling is a genius to tell
a Christian story in the unexpected disguise of a witchcraft
tale — people who would never pick up an overtly Christian story are reading Potter by the millions, attracted to it
by its modern themed packaging.

I've used C.S. Lewis and J.R.R. Tolkien to compare with
J.K. Rowling. Most readers are familiar with these authors.
They have something in common: all three are British
authors and they all write fiction. Do they have more than
that in common?

I think Lewis and Tolkien are useful comparisons: Lewis'
work is allegorical; Rowling's is not. Tolkien's is a fantasy;
Rowling's are more fairy tales. Lewis and Tolkien are dead;
Rowling is alive. Lewis and Tolkien wrote many other kinds
of books besides their fiction; Rowling hasn't had a chance
yet. I agree with Stratford Caldecott, editor of *Second
Spring*, and a director of ResSource Ltd., an educational

initiative in Oxford, England, that not every new piece of fiction or fantasy should be compared with Tolkien and Lewis.

I think it is a mistake to try to compare every work of fantasy with Tolkien's, since such works may have different jobs to do and ways of doing it. HP does in my view portray a very clear distinction between good and evil and the battle between them. The world of the "muggles" is the banal world of everyday existence. Harry's transition to the world of magic via Platform [Nine and Three Quarters] is his awakening into the inner world or spiritual battlefield — Hogwarts is his training ground. Dumbledore [is] his gentle, courteous and often surprising guru. The initiation is complex, because Hogwarts is not a pure refuge for the good, but a concentrated microcosm where good and evil are slugging it out at many levels. Harry himself has tendencies to good and evil and needs to learn discernment, among other things. Evil in its concentrated form is clearly portrayed as the desire for power over others and immortality: Voldemort's psycho-spiritual development is examined in the. . . book [Half-Blood Prince] and it is clear he has made himself evil by reject[ing] the good for the sake of those things. There is a brilliant analysis of mortal sin in the passage about "Horcruxes." The dark wizard splits his soul into fragments by the act of murder, in an attempt to attain immortality by so dividing his soul that the various fragments can be hidden where no one can find them. Pure good is portrayed as Love: self-giving, self-sacrificial love, and the acceptance of death. It was the love of Harry's mother that immunized him against Voldemort's "will to death." The adolescent Harry himself finds this teaching a bit sentimental but Dumbledore explains there is more to it than he thinks. (This is equivalent to C.S. Lewis's "deeper magic from

before the dawn of time" in The Lion the Witch and the
Wardrobe.) With the apparent death of the guru in the
[sixth] volume and the imminent closing of Hogwarts,
Harry has come of age and the battle has now moved
out into the world. The success of the whole story
depends on the resolution that will come in the next and
final volume [Harry Potter and the Deathly Hallows],
but it is clear to me that (whether or not she manages
to achieve her artistic aim) J.K. Rowling is portraying
the battle between good and evil in a way that Chris-
tians understand it, though without relying on an
explicit religious framework. Her intention is much
closer to Lewis and Tolkien than to E. Nesbit, for exam-
ple — who also preserved a moral framework but whose
aim seemed to be sheer entertainment.

— Stratford Caldecott, *The Chesterton Review*,
Fall/Winter 2005, p. 294. (Used with permission.)

People argue Rowling's books use a contemporary type
of occultism, such as astrology and divination. The three
wise men who visit Jesus followed the stars, and there is the
mention of a seer of the future in one of St. Paul's letters.
Yet, they aren't contemporary types of occultism. There is
only one class at Hogwarts school which the headmaster
and deputy headmistress seem to feel is unworthy of serious study: divination. The author, Rowling, has the students making up dreams for the dream diary they're
supposed to keep; Harry looks into his cloudy crystal ball
and tells his friend Ron there's going to be foggy weather;
the tea leaves can be turned around one way to mean one
thing, and the other to mean another. Hermione, the most
intelligent girl in the class, drops out of divination after the
teacher proclaims to everyone that Hermione has no ability to "see." Of all the made-up classes at Hogwarts,
Divination is the closest to real occultism, and it's also the
class least taken seriously in the story.

Rowling's work has been criticized for not having God in charge of the good side. Many stories are told without mentioning God, including the Prodigal Son. It isn't essential to mention God in order for a story to be good. For example, in Matthew 20:1, Jesus begins "The kingdom of God is like. . ." In a sense, every good story begins, "The kingdom of God is like. . ." if it reflects the one story, the Story of God. I believe J.K. Rowling's story could begin with, "The kingdom of God is like a school, and one of the masters is good, and one of the students was afraid of death and wanted to live forever. . . ."

Is God absent from the Potter stories? No: the most powerful force in the Harry Potter books is the self-sacrificing love of one person for another. Since God is love, God is there in each Potter book in the disguise of love.

"While such modern philosophers as Kant and Kohlberg have regarded a mother's self-sacrificing love for her children as beneath their level of morality, folk wisdom tells us it is nearly the highest morality, taking precedence over the duties of citizenship or the claims of humanity."
— Thomas Fleming, *The Morality of Everyday Life: Rediscovering an Ancient Alternative to the Liberal Tradition*, p. 9

The main point of Harry Potter: Harry is saved by the sacrificial love of his mother; saved by the sacrificial death of his mother; he's protected by love; a curse backfires to the detriment of the forces of evil. . . this is powerful stuff, serious stuff. It sounds religious. Why? Because it is.

The true object of an intelligent detective story is not to baffle the reader, but to enlighten the reader; but to

enlighten him in such a manner that each successive portion of the truth comes as a surprise.

                      — G.K. Chesterton

What Do the Bible and the *Catechism* Have to Say?

Divination and Magic

Naturally, the Bible and the *Catechism* reject all practice of divination and sorcery. Harry Potter is a fictional work, which portrays magical practices fictionally. The potion recipes are never given in full, and the ingredients mentioned are things that don't really exist. The future cannot be predicted; the past cannot be changed. No one calls on a demon for their spells; they call out Latin sounding words. If anyone tries this at home, nothing happens, as one would expect. The magic in Harry Potter is fictional, so the Bible and the *Catechism* don't condemn it. Harry Potter is a story, a work of an author's imagination, a modern-day parable. The *Catechism of the Catholic Church*, sections 2116-2117 talk about divination, and in Deuteronomy 18:9-12, going to fortune tellers and palm readers, among other things, is forbidden. The Bible and the *Catechism* reject real sorcery, and forbid us from trying to call on demons, but again, that's not what Harry Potter is — Harry Potter is a fictional story. Reading the book does not put one in danger of going against the Bible or the *Catechism*, just as attending a child's magic show does not put one in danger of being involved in "real" sorcery.

The Harry Potter Fan Club

One criticism of Rowling's books is they create "disciples" rather than book critics. The key to a fair and equal treatment of her books seems to be discovering either a) the writing is getting looser and Rowling is suffering from famous author syndrome — that is, editors no longer edit her work; or b) the magic in the story isn't as good as the

magic in other stories, such as the Edward Eager books, *Half Magic, Seven-Day Magic, Magic or Not?* or Tolkien's *The Lord of the Rings* series, or Lewis' *Narnia* series.

I don't think Rowling's books are perfect. There is, in my opinion, an over-use of bathroom and body fluids humor. I didn't enjoy reading about someone throwing up slugs. Nearly Headless Nick seems a gratuitously gory figure. An editor could have taken these out or changed them, for there is plenty of other great humor in the stories.

On the other hand, I find it amazing a children's story published in our times has no smoking or drug usage; no homosexuality or mixed up sexual feelings; no TV at school, no cable, dish, movies, internet, computers, or IMing; there is very little swearing, very little kissing, not even a token single parent family. Harry, Ron, Hermione, Draco, Seamus — in fact, all of the main children — have two parents, one male and one female. In the world of children's books today, this is unusual.

In addition, there have been plenty of Rowling fans who have pointed out inconsistencies in her magical world: things that worked one way in one book, and another in another or a certain student still present in Book Five, who should have graduated based on his age given in an earlier book. Given the sheer number of details Rowling keeps track of from book to book, it is amazing she tracks as much as she does.

One of the positive things in the books is the humor. The twins Fred and George provide constant comic relief. History class still manages to be boring. The titles of the school textbooks are humorous. The "Accidental Magic Reversal Department" is funny, and that under-17-year-olds can't magically travel from place to place until they pass their test is funny. There is joy in the humor. The idea that the latest broomsticks are faster than the older broomsticks is funny and reflects our children's interests in the latest models of their gadgets, too.

> ## More Dinner Table Questions
>
> Does Hagrid act like a parent sometimes? Give examples.
> When does Hagrid act like a child? Is it safe to tell Hagrid
> your secrets? Why does Hagrid live in a hut? Who does
> Hagrid admire the most at Hogwarts?

What I like about this novelist is that he takes such
trouble about his minor characters.

— G.K. Chesterton

Supernatural Restoration

I believe the Harry Potter books restore a sense of the
supernatural. One of the main themes in the books, and
another reason why they aren't for the very young, is death.
Harry Potter is about immortality, life after death, the
power of love, and love's effectiveness even after the person
has died; children can't fail to understand there is an afterlife in these stories and the main characters believe in it.

J.K. Rowling also does a fine job depicting a funeral at
the end of the sixth book. Again, without any hint of religion, the ceremony is thoughtful, meaningful, and full of
symbolism, with the phoenix flying upward at the end.
This could symbolize the soul's flight to heaven. Rowling
walks a fine line, considering that she's kept all traces of religion out of her books; yet she manages to hint at the beauty
of tradition, ritual, and the afterlife in this scene.

When someone very close to Harry dies in the series,
Harry is trying to work out what happened. He consults
with one of the castle ghosts, thinking perhaps his loved one
could still exist as a ghost.

When Harry can't get a straight answer out of the ghost,
he turns instead to Luna, a girl in class, whom he knows has
suffered a loss. She reminds Harry that even though their

loved ones are gone, it isn't as though they'll never see them again. This gives Harry comfort as he contemplates the loss of his loved one.

Harry can hope, if he believes, as Luna says, his loved ones are just out of sight, just beyond the "veil," that he'll see them again one day. This is a biblical reference, for in Matthew 27:51, we read, "And behold the veil of the temple was rent in two from the top even to the bottom, and the earth quaked, and the rocks were rent." The veil of the temple being split symbolizes the opening of heaven accomplished by Jesus' death, and the end of the Old Covenant, and the beginning of the New Covenant. In another place, Hebrews 6:19-20, " Which we have as an anchor of the soul, sure and firm, and which enter in even within the veil; Where the forerunner Jesus is entered for us, made a high priest for ever according to the order of Melchisedech." Entering within the "veil" is going over into the side of the physically dead but spiritually alive. The veil is a division between the living and the dead, as suggested by Luna to Harry in this scene.

Frequently, I'm asked for advice about Harry Potter problems such as this: *Last night, I told my thirteen-year-old to go to bed, but I found him with a flashlight reading Harry Potter and it was midnight! He had school the next day! The next afternoon he was crabby and short with me, and now I regret ever allowing him to read Harry Potter.*

This is a parenting issue, and not a Harry Potter issue. Yes, the books are compelling. I remember reading Nancy Drew past "lights out" in my day. However, disobedience is still disobedience. Maybe Johnny needs a few days rest from Harry Potter (or until Friday night). Think of a consequence that will be meaningful, and enforce it.

CHESTERTON

And the Pope has cast his arms abroad for agony and
*   loss,*
And called the kings of Christendom for swords
*   about the Cross*
— G.K. Chesterton, Lepanto, lines 9-10

I say to you all, once again — in light of Lord Volde-
mort's return, we are only as strong as we are united,
as weak as we are divided. Lord Voldemort's gift for
spreading discord and enmity is very great. We can
fight it only by showing an equally strong bond of
friendship and trust. Differences of habit and lan-
guage are nothing at all if our aims are identical and
our hearts are open.

*   It is my belief — and never have I so hoped that I*
am mistaken — that we are all facing dark and diffi-
cult times. Some of you in this Hall have already suf-
fered directly at the hands of Lord Voldemort. Many
of your families have been torn asunder. A week ago,
a student was taken from our midst.

*   Remember Cedric. Remember, if the time should*
come when you have to make a choice between what
is right and what is easy; remember what happened to
a boy who was good, and kind, and brave, because he
strayed across the path of Lord Voldemort.
— GF, pp. 723-724

Pope Pius V (1504-1572), the Pope Chesterton writes about
in *Lepanto*, was a Dominican monk, holy, ascetic, and can-
onized. Very different from his Renaissance predecessors, all
who came from the aristocratic class. They were some of the

most notoriously corrupt Popes in history, and under whom Christendom splintered. There was "agony and loss" within Christian Europe, but the most immediate threat came from without: the Moslem Turks (*Lepanto*, p 13). It was time for Europe to unite with strength against the invaders.

In the same way, Dumbledore, headmaster of Hogwarts School, recognizes the strength of unity against the common enemy. He reminds us of our choice — the wide and easy way — or the narrow road.

Fairy Tales

Harry Potter is considered by some to be too serious or grave. Is "Little Red Riding Hood" too intense because the wolf dresses up as Little Red's grandmother and eats her? Or "Jack and the Beanstalk" too grave because the Giant plans to eat the Englishman he smells? Or is Cain killing Abel too dark?

Stories about death are dark by their very nature. We wish to delay the time when our young children must know about death; yet, death is a part of life that all must face eventually. It may be the death of their first pet, or the death of a great-grandparent, or Good Friday church service; children can't get through childhood without a taste of death. Parents, whether they want to or not, whether they're ready or not, have to help their children deal with death.

Harry Potter doesn't bring up anything abnormal or cruel. People die; that's a part of life. In fact, I believe Harry Potter allows us to think about death in a real way, pondering its significance. Death isn't passed over, glossed over or lost in the narrative: it is a main theme. As far as most contemporary children's literature, Rowling does far more to help children deal with death than most authors.

The Bible tells the story of Jesus' crucifixion. When is a child ready to hear Jesus' story? Parents know their children

best. Parents should decide when their child is ready for Harry Potter. And just as parents wouldn't give a child a TV and say, "Here you go, have fun!" we parents need to monitor what our children are reading.

Parents bring action heroes like Spider-Man, Batman, and Superman into their children's lives, often without a second thought. Spider-Man has powers allowing him to climb walls and swing from buildings. Batman and Superman, too, use special power to save the day. We don't often hear parents complaining about the special powers in these superhero stories. Many parents read the story of King Arthur to their children, including the wizard Merlin.

As Catholics, we can use whatever God created as the means at hand for thinking about God. When I read Harry Potter, I'm contemplating moral principles about good fighting evil and I'm touching on principles I can apply to my own life. I might not absorb these principles — I have free will — but they are certainly brought to my attention. The spiritual lens through which I'm looking is my Catholic lens. And to me, that's the best way to see J.K. Rowling's creative work.

Certainly, the books can be read with a different focus: if children are already inclined to seek personal power in alternative ways, they may wander further into that world by being attracted to the "bad" characters in the Rowling novels. However, I don't believe that children of families who have raised their children with solid morals and values run that risk. Especially if they have a parent guide reading alongside them.

We must understand the nature of the novels. It is the difference between showing a child how to work out a math problem, and telling them the rule for working out that kind of problem. Harry Potter doesn't tell us the "rules;" rather, it shows us their application, or how it works out, and the consequences. There is a moral, but you have to work it out yourself, like figuring out a parable.

Questions to Ponder

1. Has your family had to deal with death yet? How did you talk to your children about death? Can the deaths of Harry's parents or any of the other characters help you to discuss death with your children?
2. What kind of a character is Harry? How does he compare with other fairy tale heroes?
3. Look up the *Catechism* and biblical references to witchcraft. How will you explain Rowling's use of magic and witchcraft to your children?
4. How will you know if your children are becoming too involved in the Harry Potter books? What signs will you watch for?

Up Next

Morality. Who even uses that old-fashioned word anymore? And what has morality to do with Harry Potter? A ton. We'll explore morality tales in the next chapter.

Chapter Four

Harry Potter and the Choice Between Good and Evil

Morality

If habits, as Aristotle says, make all the difference between virtue and vice, then the environment in which good habits are acquired is an essential aspect of moral development. For more than 99 percent of the time in which man has been developing on this planet, he has lived within the narrow orbit of families and small-scale communities. What is the point of a moral system that leaves these facts of life out of the picture?
— Fleming, *The Morality of Everyday Life*, p. 121

We must not only avoid evil but practice the good, what forming good habits is about. Harry and his friends realize they must practice defending themselves against the Dark Side, and so must we. In addition, Harry realizes there are two sides, good and bad, right and wrong, good and evil, each must choose sides; there is no balance nor compromise. As Chesterton's dying words indicate his beliefs:

The issue is now quite clear. It is between light and darkness and every one must choose his side.
— Maisie Ward, *Gilbert Keith Chesterton*, p. 50

One type of book which J.K. Rowling's Potter series is compared to is the popular Victorian English Public School stories, of which *Tom Brown's School Days* is the best exam-

ple. In the story, Tom is at first unable to live up to the high standards of the Headmaster. Yet, he transforms over the course of the series into a good student.

A Good Person Isn't a Perfect Person

Dumbledore is the main and best "good" character — the head of the Order of the Phoenix. He is very good, not infallible; he isn't God. He is the authority, he acts with gentleness and kindness, he is wise, he can get angry if the occasion calls for it, he makes mistakes, and admits them. At the end of *Order of the Phoenix*, Dumbledore says he made a mistake in withholding information from Harry.

It takes maturity to admit one's mistakes. There is no better test of a man's ultimate chivalry and integrity than how he behaves when he is wrong, says Chesterton.

We have many moral tales in our collective memory in which the name of God is not mentioned, and these are still tales we tell our children. Harry Potter is a moral tale. Our children can learn from it as from any good moral tale.

On the dark side, there's the evil Lord Voldemort, the obvious king of the bad guys — called Death Eaters. Voldemort is the head of the bad side and a Satan figure. He's chasing immortality, and seems unable to die, having now split his soul into pieces, each of which seems to be capa-

More Dinner Table Questions

Take a piece of paper, and make two columns. On the right, start listing the good characters. On the left, list the bad characters. Some will be obvious, and others will be less so, as they may seem good, but sometimes act badly. Does this put them on the right or the left? Discuss each character with your children.

ble of resurrecting itself into some form of a person, although not whole, again. Voldemort can kill with a single curse, and murders innocent victims in his quest for immortality and power. Voldemort's followers are marked with a sign, a tattoo which burns at his call; he promises them power if they do his bidding; he causes destruction wherever he or his followers go; he has all the signs of being evil personified, Lucifer himself.

Children reading the Potter books understand the nature of Voldemort's evil, as this letter to the editor of *Newsweek* magazine states:

In your Nov 26 Periscope story "Harry and Jesus" (about the new HP film) you ask "Can this movie help kids deal with the [terrorist] attacks?" My experience with my own children makes me answer "Yes". On Sep 11 my 9-year-old daughter's school had kept the students sheltered from the news all day, so as we drove home I tried to explain to her what had happened. When we pulled into our driveway, she looked up with tears in her eyes and said, "Mom, it feels like Lord Voldemort has risen." In one sentence she summed up how I had felt since 9 that morning. Two days later my 11-year-old son returned from an environmental camp in the mountains where he had been far away from TV and newspapers. I picked him up at school, not knowing exactly what he had been told about the events of the week. As we were driving home, I asked him how he had felt when he first heard about the attacks. His response shocked me, since he had not seen his sister all week. He said, "At first, I was really upset, but then I remembered what Hagrid said at the end of the 4th book." Not having memorized the HP books line for line as my children have, I had to ask, "What did Hagrid say?" His response blew me away. "What's coming will

come and we'll meet it when it does." If that's not proof
that HP has helped children process these events, what is?
— From "Letters" in *Newsweek* (Dec. 10,
2001: 18, 20), by Pamela L. Reeves,
Knoxville, TN. (Used with permission.)

Harry Potter can help children and adults to cope with evil acts such as 9/11, and help us recognize evil and call it by name. In the books most of the characters are afraid to name Voldemort. He is He-Who-Must-Not-Be-Named, and You-Know-Who to most characters, and those who do pronounce his name are hushed.

The few characters who do call Voldemort by name, though, are viewed as brave. In this way, the books help readers recognize and name evil for what it is.

The fight taking place against Voldemort is both physical and spiritual. Harry must practice closing his mind to evil's temptations and attempts at intrusions. This is not unlike we Christians, who must work to keep evil at bay. Rather than being less able to recognize evil, the books help readers to recognize evil and call it by name, thereby being better able to defeat it when it is recognized.

Harry is growing and learning; he makes plenty of mistakes along the way. When facing Voldemort, as he must do near the end of each book, he makes the right choices, puts the needs of others before his own, helps those in danger first, overcomes selfishness to do what's right and good, and acts with more strength, courage, and character than anyone else in the stories. And, as Dumbledore has reminded us, Harry's greatest strength is love.

The strongest force opposing evil in the Potter books is love. Love triumphs before the stories even begin when Lily Potter, Harry's mother, sacrifices herself to save Harry from being murdered by Voldemort as a one-year-old baby. In fact, love triumphs at the conclusion of each story in a

dramatic way. In each case, Voldemort is on the side of death and destruction, lies, villainy, and cruelty; and Harry triumphs with love, goodness, courage, selflessness, and solid moral character. There is a line in Harry Potter where Hermione says, "Wait! You can't hurt a baby!" which is a nice, subtle, pro-life message. Many people see the Weasley family, with their seven children and red hair, representing a large Irish Catholic family.

All of the other characters in the book line up either on the good or evil side of the coin — although "good" characters do occasionally confuse the reader by behaving badly. It is in the nature of a mystery novel to keep certain information veiled until the end. Characters must seem to be not quite what they are, otherwise the mystery isn't a mystery.

We are forced to think about and try to distinguish between mean and revengeful behavior, and evil behavior; we must distinguish between meanness and wickedness.

Choices and Free Will

One of the themes in this series of books is choices, or free will. As Dumbledore tells Harry near the end of *Chamber of Secrets*, our choices — far more than our abilities — show what we truly are.

There is one thing Harry doesn't seem to have a choice about: Voldemort's coming for him. Harry can't escape fighting Voldemort. Perhaps this reminds us we will face evil and sin in our lives, and we can't escape.

Harry is accused in the books of being a son of evil because he has an uncommon skill, an apparently evil gift. The students suspect that only a really powerful Dark Lord could defeat another really powerful Dark Lord, and so maybe Harry is really evil, even though he appears good.

CHESTERTON

Dim drums throbbing in the hills half heard
Where only on a nameless throne a crownless prince
*   has stirred*
Where, risen from a doubtful seat and half-attainted
*   stall,*
The last knight of Europe takes weapons from the
*   wall*

— G.K. Chesterton, Lepanto, lines 15-19

He was not going to die crouching here like a child
playing hide-and-seek; he was not going to die
kneeling at Voldemort's feet... he was going to die
upright like his father, and he was going to die trying
to defend himself, even if no defense was possible...
Before Voldemort could stick his snakelike face
around the headstone, Harry stood up... he gripped
his wand tightly in his hand, thrust it out in front of
him, and threw himself around the headstone, facing
Voldemort.

— GF, pp. 662-663

The "crownless prince" in the Lepanto poem is Don John of Austria, a youthful 25-year-old, destined to lead the defense against the dark invaders. John was the illegitimate son of the Holy Roman Emperor Charles V (1500-1558) and Barbara Blomberg of Ratisbon which was then an Austrian city, thus Don John *of Austria*. Being of royal blood, John is a prince; because he was illegitimate, he is without royal title, and has a "nameless throne."

Some people view the "good side of magic" and the "dark side of magic" in Harry Potter as similar to the Star Wars series. Star Wars speaks of the "Force" and the false

notion of a need to balance the "good side of the Force" with the "dark side of the Force." Luke is a similar character to Harry, Obi Wan Kenobi is similar to Dumbledore, even dying to save his protégé, and Lord Vader is similar to Lord Voldemort. However, in Harry Potter, as in Lepanto, there is no such balancing act: everyone must choose his side, and the good *must* win.

Harry has been taught to duel, and, like Don John of Austria, is destined to lead the fight against evil. Something in Harry's blood has saved him from the evil Lord's powerful "killing curse" and given him strength beyond that of his peers. He's chosen to lead, not knowing why. When faced with death, he recalls the sacrifice of his parents, and stands courageously facing his enemy.

This kind of thinking reminds me of this in the Bible:

And the scribes who came down from Jerusalem said, "[Jesus] is possessed by Beelzebul, and by the prince of demons he casts out the demons." And [Jesus] called [his disciples] to him, and said to them in parables, "How can Satan cast out Satan? If a kingdom is divided against itself, that kingdom cannot stand. And if a house is divided against itself, that house will not be able to stand. And if Satan has risen up against himself and is divided, he cannot stand, but is coming to an end. But no one can enter a strong man's house and plunder his goods, unless he first binds the strong man; then indeed he may plunder his house.

— Mark 3:22-27

Harry knows he isn't working *with* Voldemort, with everything inside himself he's *against* Voldemort. Even if

Harry happens to have a certain skill that looks suspicious, that doesn't mean he is working for the enemy.

More Dinner Table Questions

Why does Harry get away with his rule infractions? First year, he flies on his broomstick against school rules, and ends up on the Quidditch team, a year younger than anyone else who can play. Next year, he arrives late in a flying car, and instead of being expelled, he's simply warned. Is Harry getting special treatment? Was Draco expelled for flying *his* broom first year? Why do the teachers make exceptions?

Right vs. Wrong

Critics of Harry Potter have claimed right and wrong are blurred in the Harry Potter series. Harry or the other characters lie to get themselves out of tight spots. They defy the rules of the school to sneak around at night, find their way into the forbidden section of the library, or to leave the castle.

All of these accusations are true. As with real children, Harry and his friends are not infallible. They make mistakes, and they suffer the consequences. If Harry, Hermione and Ron were perfect characters, never lying or doing anything against the rules, they would, first, not act like real children; and second, not have any room to grow and improve. This is a morality tale, and as such, the characters need to learn to behave themselves. Which means at first, they don't know how to behave, or what's the right thing to do. They must be taught, they must grow in virtue, and they must want to succeed at becoming moral human beings.

Harry moves from being a pre-adolescent ten-year-old, to being a young adult. A lot happens in our children's pre-teen and teen years, and a lot happens to Harry.

Questions to Ponder

1. How is magic used in Rowling's story? If the good and bad characters use magic, is magic their religion? Is magic a talent? How is the magic in the story different from "real" magic — witchcraft used by those who tap into unnatural sources of power?

2. Are good and evil black and white? How do children's views of good and evil change as they grow into adulthood? Do the lines remain clear? If the lines become blurred, does it mean nothing is good or evil? Or no one can define good and evil for anyone else? Who decides what is good or evil?

3. 9/11 is an obvious example of an evil act in our day. Can you and your children think of any other acts you could describe as evil? What events in the Potter books does your family consider evil?

Up Next

Do your children have special skills and talents? Violin? Piano? An ability to memorize? Snowboard champ? Each of our children is born with special talents, and as parents we try to encourage and support our children in developing their talents. The magic in the Harry Potter books is often compared to an in-born talent. How do these two ideas compare? We'll find out in the next chapter.

Chapter Five

The Magic of Harry Potter

Why Are These Books about Magic?

A guide to help parents to discern good books for their children, *A Landscape with Dragons*, has this to say:

> *We must ask ourselves some hard questions here: If a child's reading is habitually in the area of the supernatural, is there not a risk that he will develop an insatiable appetite for it, an appetite that grows ever stronger as it is fed? Will he be able to recognize the boundaries between spiritually sound imaginative works and the deceptive ones? Here is another key point for parents to consider: Are we committed to discussing these issues with our children? Are we willing to accompany them, year after year, as their tastes develop, advising caution here, sanctioning liberality there, each of us, young and old, learning as we go? Are we willing to pray diligently for the gift of wisdom, for inner promptings from the Holy Spirit, and for warnings from guardian angels? Are we willing to sacrifice precious time to pre-read some novels about which we may have doubts? Are we willing to invest effort to help our children choose the right kind of fantasy literature from library and bookstore? Unless we are, perhaps the entire field should be left alone for a time.*
>
> — Michael O'Brien, *A Landscape With Dragons*, pp. 110-111

In our house, we have decided to do the work of pre-reading, to pray for the guidance of the Holy Spirit, to invest the time necessary to help our children develop a healthy ability to choose good books for themselves. Stories are important to children and the ability to read stories and find the good in them, using them to learn important life lessons, is an important task of childhood.

Why Are These Books about Magic?

Just why, distressed parents ask, are these books about magic? Why are the characters witches and wizards? Why do they use magic wands, and practice spells and make potions and try to harm each other with the incantations they shout? Couldn't this story be told — if there is anything to be gained from it, for example, if it *is* a moral tale — *another* way *without* magic or witchcraft?

Yes, this story could have been told another way. For example, if the story had been science fiction, and the characters used futuristic transporters to travel from place to place, or used blue liquids to fall asleep during the jump to hyper-space; or weapons such as phasers, ray guns, a photon bomb, or other high-tech weaponry, I don't think anyone would question the use of "magic."

The story could have been told using superheroes attending school, where some grow into good superheroes and others turn bad and become the villains. No one would question the student's use of his or her "superpowers."

If the story were an ancient fairy tale, and magic beans were used to grow a vine to the giant, and a magic harp were used to lull a three-headed dog to sleep, I don't think anyone would complain.

If the story were a myth, and the bad guy was looking for the magic stone that allows him to live forever, and the good guy was trying to stop the bad guy from finding the

know there are good and bad witches. Samantha, the mother in the story Bewitched, and Tabitha, her daughter, did not grab our attention because they were witches doing magic in a non-magical world; they caught our attention because they were people dealing with their everyday lives in humorous ways. The TV screenplay was not written to endorse witchcraft or wizardry, it was written to provide children and adults entertainment.

There is something missing in my generation. I find it interesting in the Harry Potter fan book *The Plot Thickens. . . Harry Potter Investigated*, written after the first five books were published, that there are dozens and dozens of fan authors. One would suspect these would be teens, or young twenty-somethings. I was surprised to see how many authors were of my generation, the 40-somethings. The same holds true on a lot of the Internet fan sites. What we are finding in Harry resonates with us.

A Review of Some Fairy Stories

Harry Potter has been criticized for using magic, for being prideful, breaking rules, going against authority and being a poor role model for our children to read about. I thought I might take a brief look at some of our most well-known fairy tales and see how the story and its hero measure up to Harry. But first, let's look at Jesus.

Jesus told stories to his disciples. Jesus knows our hearts respond to stories, so he uses them to teach us how to live, and how to change our lives. Jesus told a story once about a father who had two boys. The younger of the two wanted his inheritance and he left home. He squandered his money on loose living and gambling. Now this boy doesn't sound much like a good role model at this point in his life, does he? Are we going to argue that Jesus is telling a bad story to us because the younger son isn't a good role model? Jesus knows how to tell a good story.

Jack, Red, and Beauty

Since Harry Potter is English, I'll begin with an English folk tale: "Jack and the Beanstalk." Jack begins by disobeying his mother and selling the cow for magic beans. Jack then steals the Giant's money, which he and his mother live off for months. When the money runs out, Jack returns to steal a magic hen which lays golden eggs, and a magic harp which sings by itself. After killing the giant, Jack and his mother live happily ever after on the wealth of the stolen hen's eggs, and on the music of the magic harp. Jack has learned not to take magic beans from strangers, but has had an advantage in growing them.

I haven't heard anyone complain if there was a good side of the magic beans and a bad side, whether or not God or Satan was the power behind the magic beans, whether or not it was right to steal from an Englishman-eating Giant. Or whether or not he should benefit from the poor giant's death. Or whether or not someone sensitive to the occult would see the occult in this story.

I believe Harry Potter is subject to these kinds of scrutinies because the stories are fresh, and haven't stood the test of time; and J.K Rowling is still alive. "Jack and the Beanstalk" and the other fairy tales have been around for centuries. Perhaps when they first came out they were criticized as well. Now, they are just part of legend, part of our human history.

In "Little Red Riding Hood," Red trusts a wolf and tells him where her grandmother lives — disobeying her mother in the process. She's in deep trouble when the wolf eats her grandmother and then poses as the sick old lady so he can eat Red. A woodsman comes along and kills the wolf, and from his insides, out comes Grandmother and Little Red who thank the woodsman for rescuing them. Little Red Riding Hood has learned not to trust wolves ever again — and never to disobey her mother.

More Dinner Table Questions

The Sorcerer's Stone, or Philosopher's Stone as it is really called (Scholastic changed the title and the name of the stone, thinking American's wouldn't buy a book they thought was about "philosophy") is a mythical stone which can make a person live forever. People have always searched for a kind of "Fountain of Youth." Why do some people want to live forever? Are they afraid of growing old? Of death?

What other books have you read where a character wants to live forever?

stone, and they ended up fighting, I don't think we'd hear a complaint.

Why does the author, J.K. Rowling, use magic and witchcraft and make the whole story confusing? The story seems to take place not in an ancient fairy tale or mythological times, not in a futuristic science fiction era, but in our own times.

Deeper meaning resides in the fairy tales told me in my childhood than in any truth that is taught in life.
— Johann Christoph von Schiller,
German Poet (1759-1805)

J.K. Rowling is quite well versed in mythology, fairy tales, ancient stories, Greek and Roman gods and goddesses, and forms of literature. She had a whole slew of choices when she started writing her story about Harry Potter. She chose to use the literary device of witchcraft and magic. Why? Children are becoming bewitched into false "good" type magic books; books with popular titles such as *The Little Green Witch* by Barbara Barbieri McGrath, *Little Witch's Bad Dream*, by Deborah Hautzig and Sylvie Wickstrom,

The Witch's Handbook, and *A Field Guide to Magic*, by Rachel Dickinson, Timothy Crawford, Paul Kepple, found in the local library and the big chain book stores.

Is There Such a Thing as a "Good" Witch?

The "good witch" books are popular. You don't see a book in the local bookstore's front window called "How to Become a Truly Great Morally Upright and Physically Chaste Teen Christian!" or "Prayers and Promises for Attracting a Date for Catholic Teens." They aren't hip and happening, they aren't slick, cool, in, rad, brilliant, wicked, or groovy.

Wicked Is *In*

What's *in* is wicked. Yes, even the word for "cool" nowadays reflects society's interest in witchcraft.

The second reason I believe Rowling uses the world of witches and wizards, is that by presenting a good story in disguise, she has the capability of luring millions of readers to her stories, who find a traditional moral tale, a tale which has no bones about spelling out what's good and what's evil.

Rowling gives us clues the stories are not about magic. For example, the magic wands in the story have a magical core which makes them functional. The magic core does not exist in our world: a phoenix feather, the hair from the tail of a unicorn, or a dragon heart-string.

> *"In a utilitarian age, of all other times, it is a matter of grave importance that fairy tales should be respected."*
> — Charles Dickens,
> British novelist (1812-1870)

Then there are the incantations, which are often simply Latin or Latin-sounding words or phrases. The potion recipes are never given wholly, and the ingredients

CHESTERTON

In that enormous silence, tiny and unafraid,
Comes up along a winding road the noise of the
Crusade

— G.K. Chesterton, *Lepanto*, lines 21-22

Standing against the ramparts, very white in the face,
Dumbledore still showed no sign of panic or distress.
He merely looked across at his disarmer and said,
"Good evening, Draco."

— HBP, p. 584

In the calm before the storm of the battle, the brave band of soldiers under the watchful eye of Don John, prepares to meet their foe and fate. In the Harry Potter books, Dumbledore is the picture of peacefulness, even when he is faced with death. And yet, under his peaceful exterior, lies strength and a fearlessness that is the basis for a life of faith and goodness, a life of fortitude and patience, a life of doing what's right.

mentioned are non-existent, such as the stone from a goat's stomach, powdered horn of a unicorn, dragon liver and so forth. Many times, the descriptions of the magical elements are humorous elements in the story.

In addition, if the characters were truly magic folk, they should be able to use magic to solve all their problems, and they can't. Harry, Percy, Dumbledore, McGonagall, and Mr. Weasley still wear glasses to see clearly. Magic is Rowling's fictional name for "human ability," neither good nor bad, except as to how one *chooses* to use it. The students must study and learn how to use their talents and skills for a pur-

pose. And does any child fail to recognize the Harry Potter stories as stories? Does any child read "Jack and the Beanstalk" and begin to wonder if they can use magic beans to solve their problems?

Real witches, wizards and magic are not tame or harmless. Real witchcraft is evil and to be avoided. Real witchcraft is nothing to be dabbled in. And there are those who, without guidance, may go astray reading Harry Potter. There are those who, without guidance, could go astray reading *The Lord of the Rings*, or even the Bible, if one picks out only certain sentences. The key to Harry Potter then is not to ban the book from the possibility of one person going astray because they read it, but to offer guidance, which is what *The Mystery of Harry Potter* is all about.

> *"If you want your children to be intelligent, read them fairy tales. If you want them to be more intelligent, read them more fairy tales."*
> — Albert Einstein, Scientist (1879-1955)

Magical Talent

If magic is to be compared to anything in the Potter books, it might be best described as a talent some have, and others don't. This talent is inborn, or it isn't, you can't become magical just by wanting to. In this way, too, the books can't be said to encourage witchcraft, when we all know people haven't been born with the magical talent the fictional characters in the Rowling books have.

The talent for magic, like talents in our world, must be developed and nurtured, or it won't do much. In addition, like real talents, fictional magic can be used for good or for evil. This could be compared to a doctor who uses his talent to either deliver or kill a baby; or an artist who can paint a beautiful picture or make pornography.

Do you think I am trying to weave a spell? Perhaps I am; but remember your fairy tales. Spells are used for breaking enchantments as well as inducing them. And you and I have need of the strongest spell that can be found to wake us from the evil enchantment of worldliness which has been laid upon us for nearly a hundred years.

— C.S. Lewis, *The Weight of Glory and Other Addresses* (New York: Collier, 1970), p. 7

J.K. Rowling is using the idea of magic to tell her story. She isn't encouraging children to learn magic and try out spells on each other. She is encouraging children to learn to be good, and try to be courageous in the face of fear. Perhaps Rowling is weaving a spell to wake us up out of our current malaise of indifferentism toward what is wrong and evil.

Questions to Ponder

1. Why are today's children attracted to "witch" books?
2. Would the Harry Potter books still be the same if told as a science fiction story? In an old-fashioned fairy tale story?
3. What evidence can you find for magic that doesn't "work" properly in the Potter books? In my example, Harry can't seem to get along without his glasses. Why couldn't his eyes be magically fixed?

Up Next

Do you have any persistent sins in your life? Sins that have become habits? How about temptations? Wouldn't you like at least a couple of them to stop being a problem for once? How do we fight the sin and temptation in our lives? Do we even think about them? When was the last time you went to confession? Sins and temptations are real, and we're going to talk more about them in the next chapter. Let's remember what Pope John Paul II used to say, "Be not afraid."

Chapter Six

Harry Potter and the Practice of Free Will

Practicing Defense Against the Dark Arts

Hang on, why would witches and wizards need to *practice* defense against the dark arts? If everything they do, as critics claim, were a dark art, there'd be no need. In the Hogwarts world, there is a battle going on and the good side must fight against the bad. Just as soldiers need to practice their battle skills, so must the students at Hogwarts practice to fight their enemy.

If we look at the Dark Arts as J.K. Rowling intended, evil uses of magic, and we compare the Dark Arts to sin and temptation, then we know we need to do something to prevent their intrusion in our lives. Do we fight sin? Resist temptation? Do we practice the skills needed to overcome the black or dark tendencies in our lives? Or do we operate as if we can go about our daily lives, and, magically, our sins and temptations will go away with no effort on our part?

More Dinner Table Questions

Dumbledore says the students may have to choose between what is right and what is easy. Why didn't he say what is right and what is wrong? Or what is hard and what is easy? Is it always hard to do what's right? Is the easy way always the wrong way? When is it hard for Harry to do what's right? Think of some examples of situations in your life where it was hard to do what was right.

What are we teaching our children? Are we teaching them how to fight life's battles, or are we indulging them by allowing them to play and socialize without learning the responsibilities of putting others first, of putting work before play — in other words, developing their character — which is more important than exuding a positive self-esteem?

Are we arming our children with weapons for the world's battle? Will knowing how to play the latest video game help them fight off sin and temptation? Do they know how to delay gratification? Save up for things they desire? Will playing on the travel hockey team teach them how to fight off selfishness?

Another point about practicing: even though Harry has skills at flying and playing Quidditch, a wizarding game similar to soccer or basketball on broomsticks, he still practices the game and works at improving his skills. This is another lesson for us who have certain God-given talents and skills. We, too, must practice our skills and hone them for the work we must do to build up the kingdom.

Fighting Sin and Temptation

The Dark Arts lessons represent fighting to resist sin and temptation in our lives. One allegorical element of Tolkien's "One Ring" is its power of temptation — characters fight over it, and must work out what to do with it. In Lewis's work, the children must figure out how to release Narnia from the grasp of the evil White Witch.

Natural Law

One element the books presume is a strict moral code of conduct: there is a right and wrong, and judgments are possible regarding actions. The books envision a world — a magical world — governed by strict rules of conduct, where actions may be good, neutral or so evil as to be "unforgivable."

Interior to each of us is this sense of right and wrong. Even without faith, we can discover "natural law" which flows out of human reason. Natural law tells us, just as the Ten Commandments do, murder is wrong; we should obey our elders, we shouldn't lie, shouldn't steal, we should be content with what we have. And our society has been bent on a course to expel the moral code from our lives.

Our modern society says nothing is wrong. If you say something is wrong you are judging, you are an intolerant, whatever-phobic, and prejudiced. And even though people buy into that, because they don't want anyone to feel badly about their choices, we know, deep in our hearts, certain things are wrong.

Schools today are working on tenterhooks. They have a hard time saying the word "mom and dad," because so many children have adult caretakers, guardians, foster families, or gender issues with the terms mom and dad. It is passing judgment to say a child should have a mother and a father, even though nature dictates it.

In the midst of all this political correctness, this tolerant, non-judgmental, relativistic world, enters a story about a school where right and wrong are defined, rules enforced, misbehavior comes with detention, evil is evil and must be fought, and goodness is rewarded. And millions of people are buying these books. Why? It is feeding a need. There is something inside us that wants to see the bad guy defeated. That wants the good rewarded. That wants the rules enforced. That wants a moral universe we can understand and live in.

Not everyone likes the Potter books. I asked a young single woman who worked at a big chain bookstore what she thought of the stories. She read the first one, and she felt, at the end, Harry should have solved his own problems, fought his own fight. I liked the fact that Harry needed a grown-up's help. She felt he was just a lucky kid and the adult saved him in the end.

Being a child of the 1980s, this young woman had been taught children were powerful and strong, and children's literature reflects this. Have you noticed how many children's books have no adults in them? The children must solve all their own problems. This may appeal to certain children's literary book specialists, but it isn't natural, and it isn't normal. Children need the guidance of parents especially; also of other trustworthy adults.

Harry must and does rely on adults in the Potter stories — one of the features that appeals to me. I want my children to read books where adults are helpful and strong, and make a positive difference in a child's life. This is unlike most of today's children's literature, where the adults are weak, stupid, absent, abusive, or negligent.

Is Harry Potter Just a Lucky Kid?

Harry is so lucky he has the most evil creature in the entire universe determined to kill him. And then there's the lucky incident where his parents are murdered and Harry is sent to live with an aunt and uncle who treat him with contempt. Yes, what a lucky guy.

The boy has an amazing amount of character to live through these ordeals and still use his talents for good. How many of us might sit around feeling sorry for ourselves and go on about what the world owes poor pitiful us? It's amazing Harry isn't more scarred than a lighting bolt on his forehead, by the incidents of his youth. Today's literary anti-hero would be a bundle of baggage, nervous, weak, and needing counseling to recover from such a traumatic youth.

Harry *is* lucky in that he has good friends around him, who help him and stick by him through the bad times. He has a great mentor in Professor Dumbledore. Harry is like us. Everyone has both good and bad things happen. What matters is how we react to them.

Does Harry Potter Get Adults to Solve His Problems?

Harry doesn't use adults to solve his problems. Harry learns from the adults around him. Because his parents were killed, Harry must rely on other adults for help and advice. In his first few years at school, Harry discovers which adults show care and concern for him and who tells the truth and gives him guidance. Harry must trust these adults because he is a child — and needs help. As he grows, he is able to recall the advice and guidance he stored in his memory and matures into an independent young adult, just as we hope our children will. We hope we've prepared our children for life's battles, given them guidance in the form of advice, armor, weapons, and all manner of defense against the dark arts.

What makes Harry Potter different from other modern books? For one thing, respect for adults. Harry calls everyone by his or her proper name, and when he slips and calls his professor "Snape," Dumbledore or Mrs. Weasley correct him and say, "*Professor* Snape." In addition, there is mutual respect among the teachers, and from teacher to student. The teachers often call Harry "Mr. Potter" and Hermione "Miss Granger."

Harry wasn't re-written to eliminate helpful adults: another reason Harry Potter slipped past the "watchful dragons" (see page 35).

The Importance of Being Parents

Harry kneaded his forehead with his knuckles. What he really wanted (and it felt almost shameful to admit it to himself) was someone like — someone like a parent: *an adult wizard whose advice he could ask without feeling stupid, someone who cared about him. . .*

— GF, p. 22

CHESTERTON

Stiff flags straining in the night-blasts cold
In the gloom black-purple, in the glint old-gold
Torchlight crimson on the copper kettle-drums
Then the tuckets, then the trumpets, then the can-
    non, and he comes
         — *G.K. Chesterton,* Lepanto, *lines 25-28*

"We're coming with you, Harry," said Neville.
    "Let's get on with it," said Ron firmly.
    Harry still did not want to take them all with
him, but it seemed he had no choice. He turned to
face the door and walked forward. Just as it had in
his dream, it swung open and he marched over the
threshold, the others at his heels.
         — *OP, pp. 769-770*

As the resistance men prepare for battle, they fortify themselves with standards — flags of their country — torchlight,
drumbeats, a flourish of trumpets, and then the cannons;
ready to fight the enemy wherever they will meet. Harry and
his band of friends must now face the enemy: Lord Voldemort, prepared by their work practicing Defense against the
Dark Arts lessons, sticking together, and mustering up all the
courage they have. Voldemort is the darkest of the dark wizards, a wizard who went as bad as one could go. There is no
question that they must fight him, and win.

When I recently watched *Charlie and the Chocolate Fac-*
tory, I noticed Willy Wonka couldn't pronounce the word
parents. He's having psychological issues. What it brought to
mind was parents count for very little in our culture: they

seem to be nearly obsolete. Caregivers, guardians, and various types of mixed adults living together often substitute for a solid set of two parents. And it's nice when a book like Harry Potter and a movie like *Charlie and the Chocolate Factory* make a big deal out of children needing and wanting parents.

Not only is Harry respectful to the adults in his life, he must rely on them for help, knowledge, history questions, and advice. Before the first story even begins, Voldemort has murdered Harry's parents. Yet, James and Lily Potter are present in every book, helping Harry. Harry's desire to know and emulate his parents, and especially his father, is a wonderful quality in the books.

Readers have described the families in Harry Potter as dysfunctional and stated today's children can relate to the story, as so many have broken or remixed families; they relate to Harry's lack of parents. Even though Harry has lost his parents, and his aunt and uncle never become a loving substitute, Harry isn't bitter, and he builds up a family of his own choosing. At Hogwarts, Dumbledore is like Harry's wise, grandfatherly mentor and guide; Sirius Black, a godfather who advises him; Ron, Hermione, Neville, Dean, and Seamus as siblings; and Lupin is a confidant and friend. Many of Harry's helpers are male, another aspect of the books that I find likeable.

"When I examine myself and my methods of thought, I come to the conclusion that the gift of fantasy has meant more to me than any talent for abstract, positive thinking."
— Albert Einstein, Scientist (1879-1955)

I recommend the literary analysis of the many books in the bibliography. If the reader is interested, excellent descriptions and explanations of the Harry Potter books are found in John Granger's *Looking for God in Harry Potter.*

The Dark Mark and the Dark Arts

The Dark Mark appears on the forearms of Voldemort's followers. The mark stings or throbs when the evil Lord calls his disciples. What about this "dark mark"? Here is something interesting from the Bible.

> *"And it was given him to give life to the image of the beast, and that the image of the beast should speak; and should cause, that whosoever will not adore the image of the beast, should be slain. Also it causes all, both small and great, both rich and poor, both free and slave, to be marked on the right hand or the forehead. . ."*
>
> — Revelation 13:15-16

Evil leaves a mark. Cain is marked in the Bible, after killing his brother. Evil leaves a scar. Even those who reform, who convert, who give up their evil ways, still have the memory of the past. We know even though God forgives our sins, and He may even forget them, it is hard for us to forget what we've done in the past. Our sins remain with us, even when forgiven, and this is a difficult burden to bear. With Christ, we don't bear it alone, and it becomes endurable.

> *"If you happen to read fairy tales, you will observe that one idea runs from one end of them to the other — the idea that peace and happiness can only exist on some condition. This idea, which is the core of ethics, is the core of the nursery-tales."*
>
> — G. K. Chesterton, *All Things Considered*

Just as our culture dictates books for children in which the children solve all their own problems, another message our world sends children is they should be themselves, act

naturally, "just do it," whatever "it" is. Sex? *Use a condom* (wink). Drink? *Do it responsibly* (wink). Don't feel like attending church with us? *Well, we don't want to force you.* Teacher says you talk out of turn too much? *Teacher doesn't understand you, sweetkins. We'll get you a new teacher.*

The message: no child should have to master himself. No child should have to practice holding his tongue or waiting his turn. Children shouldn't have to control their impulses; they should be allowed to be free to do whatever they desire.

Although many parents and teachers don't agree with this one hundred percent, they send the unspoken message and then wonder why their children aren't in control. The school doesn't expect teens to control their physical bodies when it comes to swearing, kissing in the hallways, or sex; they do expect teens to control their thoughts and their speech, toeing the politically correct line on global warming, the blessings of Planned Parenthood and the evils of homophobia. Children are smart enough to learn the rules, and they realize at times they must be in control, other times they won't be expected to. Teens view adults as weak for being unable to enforce or even teach moral rules and guidelines. And we are if we don't.

Practice Using Free Will

Just because a wizard doesn't use Dark magic doesn't mean he can't. . .

— CS, p. 152

This emphasis on free will, and having the strength to resist exercising power, even if we have the power, is another one of the great messages of Harry Potter.

In Rowling's books, the Hogwarts students are expected to obey the rules, rule breaking costs the school houses

points, or puts them in detention — they must speak respectfully to the teachers, their parents are involved in the school and get letters sent home when a student is out of line. The students must practice the things they are learning in order to defend themselves against the enemies. The students have free will and must make choices, based on what side they decide to follow. Children like this. They can't get enough of Harry Potter. They really want this kind of order in their lives.

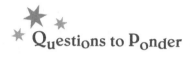

Questions to Ponder

1. The Hogwarts students must practice Defense Against the Dark Arts. What daily things do you do to defend yourself against the "Dark Arts"? What practices can you teach your children? (Examples: daily Scripture reading as a family, rosary and prayers, blessing the children before bed, etc.)

2. Do you have a set of house rules? What happens if the rules are broken?

3. Do your children call adults by their proper names, such as Mr. and Mrs. Smith? People think this is a quaint old-fashioned idea, what do you think? Why might it be important for children to call adults by their proper names?

Up Next

When was the last time you read a fairy tale? Do your children like Cinderella? Robin Hood? King Arthur? Is Harry Potter a fairy tale? Let's find out in the next chapter.

Chapter Seven

Harry Potter and the Modern Morality Tale

A Fairy Tale

Harry Potter is a fairy tale set in modern times. Perhaps if the story had been set in the 1800s or the 1300s, no one would question the use of witches and wizards as characters. Perhaps it would have been obvious that the stories are fairy tales.

And why does our world need new fairy tales? Don't we have enough fairy tales already? "Cinderella," "Jack and the Beanstalk," "Hansel and Gretel," aren't these enough? Do storytellers have to come up with new fairy tales for each generation?

They don't *have* to. Stories like "Cinderella" and "Hansel and Gretel" can still weave their magic tales and teach children about the world, but there are aspects of them a child of today might not be able to understand. A newer fairy tale might speak to a child of the 21st century in a way an older story may not. Yes, updated fairy tales might have a place in our world.

The grounds were very dark now; the only light came from the distant windows of the castle.

— PA, p. 380

Do J.K. Rowling's stories qualify as fairy tales? Certainly, they do. Transportation by broom sticks, flying cars, three-headed-dogs, a castle on a hill with turrets and towers, and an evil villain every bit as evil as the witch who gave Sleeping Beauty her poisoned apple — such classic fairy tale

elements as these are what elevate Harry Potter above the ordinary. G.K. Chesterton heard a fairy tale, *The Princess and the Goblin* by George MacDonald, when he was little, and he was profoundly affected. He later said it made all the difference to his life.

Though new philosophies come and go, it is still true the "goblins under the floor" are there inside our "house"; the house being our souls, at home in our bodies, and the goblins being sin and temptations which try to besiege us from below. Besieging us from below can refer to concupiscence, the condition in which we all live, where our souls yearn for good, but our physical sensations, our natural inclinations, our "lower appetites" must be brought into right order, into obedience with our minds and hearts through the use of reason. This is a war we battle all our lives. (See article on concupiscence at www.newadvent.org/cathen/04208a.htm.)

The Post-Baby-Boomer-Flower-Power-Me Generation

My generation, born in the 1960s, growing up in the 1970s, did not grow up with Grimm's fairy tales. We grew up with the Partridge Family and the Brady Bunch. We are a TV generation. We grew up with *Bewitched* and *The Wizard of Oz*. We did not need Harry Potter to come along and confuse us about "good" witches and "bad" witches, we already

---

More Dinner Table Questions

When Harry gets his first magic wand, he finds out that the magical inner core is a phoenix feather, and the phoenix only gave one other, and it's in the wand of Voldemort. The phoenix also happens to be Dumbledore's pet, Fawkes. How are these three characters related? Does the phoenix feather help the owner in some way? How are Harry and Voldemort alike? How are they different, and why are they different?

In "Beauty and the Beast," we see an obedient daughter who does her father's wishes. In the castle of the beast, by the way, is a magic mirror in which Beauty can see her home and her father, not unlike the Mirror of Erised in Harry Potter. Beauty's ability to love the Beast, despite his ugliness, breaks the spell and turns him into the person he is: a handsome prince. Someone had to love him for his goodness alone to break the spell.

I think we can see from these few examples that Harry Potter fits into the realm of fairy story, with similar elements. To criticize the magic and witchcraft in Harry Potter is similar to saying there shouldn't be magic beans in "Jack and the Beanstalk," or a magic mirror in "Beauty and the Beast," when that is part of the fairy tale, and not a story promoting the use of magic in everyday normal human life.

Cinderella's fairy godmother doesn't say whether her powers to transform Cinderella come from goodness or evil; we understand their goodness from the resulting beauty. No one says, after reading Cinderella, "there is no good use of magic. This story must be evil."

> *Don't mention it to anyone else unless you find that they've had adventures of the same sort themselves. What's that? How will you know? Oh, you'll know all right. Odd things they say — even their looks — will let the secret out. Keep your eyes open. Bless me, what do they teach them at these schools?*
>
> — Professor, *The Lion, The Witch, and the Wardrobe*, p. 189

Morality in Fiction

In Thomas Fleming's book, *The Morality of Everyday Life*, he argues morality is historically not black and white, but "casuistry", which he says is the very opposite of modern

day moralists. They think of morality as a kind of arithmetic or algebra, a formula is applied to any or every situation. Instead, morality, according to Fleming, "is more like ecology in refusing to divorce organisms from their interactions both with each other and with their environment."

In other words, modern moralists would like every situation in a category. "Lying is always wrong," they might say. The post-modern moralists, on the other hand, would probably say, "Lying is never really wrong." Whereas the ancient moralists and Fleming argue that we moderns — if we think about it — understand there are circumstances where not telling the complete truth might save a life. Or, as the *Catechism* says, not revealing the truth to its fullest might be a better option than the full truth in some circumstances. The *Catechism* sees truth on a scale with fully revealed completely disclosed truth on one side, and nothing revealed on the other, and tells us that it is for us to determine where along that continuum we should reveal truth, based on the circumstance. (*Catechism*, paragraphs 2464-2513, but especially 2469: Truthfulness keeps to the just mean between what ought to be expressed and what ought to be kept secret: it entails honesty and discretion.)

If faced with the question, "Did you take that cookie?" the guilty party should fully reveal the truth, "Yes, I did." If faced with the question, "Did you hide a priest here?" the guilty party could say, "Priest! What priest? What are you

---

Never Too Late

If your childhood was filled with TV instead of fairy tales, it isn't too late. Reading "classic" literature and old-fashioned fairy tales is never out of style. Instead of watching Oprah this afternoon, open up a good, classic book and begin reading. Our imaginations are exercised, even if we're long past childhood.

talking about? Do I look like the kind of person who would hide a priest?" He hasn't revealed the truth because he's trying to save the priest's life. Not revealing the truth in an attempt to save an innocent life is not wrong to the same degree it is wrong if a person withheld information about his marital status, for example, to an interested party of the opposite sex.

Cause-You-Is-What?

Harry Potter, besides being a fairy tale, is a moral tale. Morality isn't discussed in our society. Talking about morality might lead to intolerance, or worse, judgmentalism; or even worse, defining right and wrong. Stories like Harry Potter teach us morality. As Thomas Fleming states in his book, *The Morality of Everyday Life*:

> *Catholic casuistry (**kaw**-zhoo-i-stree, case-based reasoning) had its classical moment in the eighteenth century, when rigorist Jansenists contended against what they regarded as the moral laxity of the Jesuits. The compromise position, often referred to as probabilism, was elaborated by St. Alphonsus Maria de Liguori (1696-1787) whose Theologia Moralis was regarded for nearly two centuries as the standard manual on casuistry. . . St. Alphonsus, who had initially been attracted to the harshness and severity of the Jansenists, eventually learned that ordinary human beings could not live up to so austere a standard. Rejecting absolutism as both impractical and, in this human world, impossible, he argued from the basis of probability, always making allowances for human frailty. The result of his method is a mature and humane approach to moral problems that has never been equaled.*

In other words, morality cannot be understood as a mathematical formula. The situation must be considered. Just as we learn that although murder is always wrong, so a priest, in a confessional, seeks to discover whether the murderer was in his right mind, knew what he was about to do and gave full consent. In the same way, our court system judges murder in different ways: first degree, second degree, manslaughter, accidental, and so forth. This involves the virtue of prudence. During our crisis moment, when we must choose, we pause a moment to reflect, trying to discern the good in each circumstance. More than just common sense, this is prudence (www.newadvent.org/cathen/12517b.htm).

> *By the beginning of the eighteenth century, Protestant Europe and North America had embraced the universal moral abstractions of Locke and Leibniz, which eliminated, so it was thought, the need for analyzing particular relationships and particular cases. During the same century, however, English novelists. . . were treating the moral complexities of everyday life with the respect they deserve. Small wonder that ordinary people preferred to take their moral instruction from [a novel] rather than from Locke's political and psychological treatises on government.*
>
> — Fleming, pp. 10-11

Even as casuistry was losing favor in the eighteenth century, the time period saw a rise in the popularity of fiction. In these novels, complex "casuistry" moral situations could be discussed and described. Their popularity describes a resonance in the hearts of the common man and woman.

> *Although casuistry fell into disgrace at the end of the seventeenth century, our need for such an approach has never gone away. In fact, ordinary people have not*

turned to moral philosophers for enlightenment but to novelists, essayists, and advice columnists. At the very time fiction came to be taken seriously as something more than light entertainment, casuistry was being extinguished by moral rationalism, and as noted, ever since the eighteenth century, people have referred to great novels as the framework for moral discussion. . .

— Fleming, p. 15

Morality Banished to the World of Fiction

Novels serve a place in our world; perhaps one of the only places where morality is discussed in the 21st century. Literature is important not only for our society, but for the church, too.

Even the most popular fiction may have lessons to teach, as G.K. Chesterton argued in defense of "penny dreadfuls." There is nothing inherently wrong with escapist fiction, if the world into which we escape is filled with heroism and honor. For some children growing up in troubled families, a good story may be more than escape: it can be a contact with a better world.

— Fleming, p. 15

Peter Kreeft, professor of philosophy at Boston College, was asked by an interviewer, "Is the study of literature important for the church?" to which he answered:

It is crucial — absolutely crucial. We are still deeply influenced by stories. We learn morality more from stories than from anything else. If we're not good storytellers, and if we're not sensitive to good storytellers, we'll miss out on the most powerful means of enlightening ourselves and

More Dinner Table Questions

The Dementors are evil characters in the book that suck out all your laughter and joy. To deflect them, Harry must think of a happy thought and call on a "patron"; in our lives, the sin against hope is despair, which takes away all our joy and laughter. To fight against despair, we must think of all we have, be grateful, and we could call on a patron saint for help. Patron is also similar to the word *Pater*, or Father, and when we cry out "Our Father" it is very much like Harry calling out *Expecto Patronum!* — "I expect my Patron!" St. Joseph's official title in the church is *Confessoris et Ecclesiae Universalis Patroni* (Confessor and Patron of the Universal Church). How does the method in which Harry deflects the Dementors compare to praying when we are down, depressed, or have lost hope?

transforming our world apart from a living, personal example.

Christianity has always produced great writers. But, unfortunately, I cannot name a single great one who is alive today. Walker Percy and Flannery O'Connor may be the two last great Christian writers. I'm sure there will be more, because it is in our tradition.

— Peter Kreeft, "Baptism of the Imagination"

This explains several things. It shows why the Harry Potter novels are so very, very popular. They show us better than anything else today how to live a moral life. The novels show a deep complexity in the choices we must make. Although there is a clear delineation between the good and evil, there are many times when we must choose greater goods over lesser goods, and we must be able to weigh complex issues.

We Are Influenced by Stories

Literature is important for the church because we humans love stories, we respond to stories. From babyhood on, children want adults to tell them stories. We are influenced by stories. We learn more about morality from stories than anywhere else. Christianity produces great storytellers

CHESTERTON

Holding his head up for a flag of all the free.
Love-light of Spain — hurrah!
Death-light of Africa!
Don John of Austria
Is riding to the sea.
　　　　— G.K. Chesterton, Lepanto, lines 31-35

Dumbledore stood aside and Harry climbed carefully into the boat. Dumbledore stepped in, too. . .
　　　　— HBP, p. 565

The battle of Lepanto was a sea battle, ships meeting ships. The image of a battle at sea is often evoked to describe our individual battles with the "enemies" — usually within. Wouldn't we like to "loose the cannonade" against our desire to oversleep, overeat or overindulge? Shoot an arrow through our tendency to gossip? Plunge a dagger into our laziness? If only it were so simple to extract the sins from our lives.

Harry and Dumbledore embark on their own journey, attempting to destroy the bits and pieces of evil that Lord Voldemort left behind to cause death and destruction. The journey is dangerous, frightening, and ultimately, deadly.

because once one knows "The" story; there are plenty of variations on a theme, if one has a good imagination.

In many ways, Harry Potter is a story for our times. Troubled children in divorced homes, foster homes, absent parent homes, can relate to Harry's lack of parents and use of substitute adults in his life. As wonderful as these other books are, Harry Potter is much more of a story for our times than either *Narnia* or *The Lord of the Rings*. The lack of parental authority in the Harry Potter books may indeed reflect the lack in our society. The substitution of other adults who care about Harry may just be a good suggestion to the children who read the books to look for good adult guides for themselves.

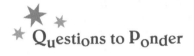

Questions to Ponder

1. What purpose does reading fairy tales to children serve?
2. What goblins are under your house?
3. If we failed to develop a moral imagination in our own childhood, what can we do now to rectify that situation?
4. Do your children have trusted non-parental adults in their lives to turn to when they have questions, need advice, guidance or help?

Up Next

"Make new friends, but keep the old. One is silver and the other gold." I still remember singing this little song in fourth grade Girl Scouts. It isn't easy to keep old friends, and it isn't easy to make new friends. But friends, we all know, are important. We'll talk more about friendship in our next chapter.

Chapter Eight

The Importance of Friendships in Harry Potter

Friendship

Harry does not navigate through trials and tribulations alone at Hogwarts. He has two faithful student friends who always help him, Ron and Hermione. Besides them, he has a host of regular confidants, including Dumbledore, Hagrid, his godfather, Lupin, and Moody. These friendships form a surrogate family. When Harry must act, he always does better when his friends are helping him. He also does better when he *listens* to his friends and takes their advice. The loyalty of the friends is an important theme.

The three friends together can be thought of as symbolizing the Trinity, Father, Son and Holy Spirit; or another way is the three aspects of the person: mind or intellect (Hermione), body (Ron), and heart (Harry). This literary device of separating the three elements, body, mind, and spirit or heart with three characters who each emphasize one of these elements is commonly used in fiction writing.

John Granger has interesting ideas in *Looking for God in Harry Potter* about the three friends and what they may represent.

> *Man is most obviously an image of God in that his soul is three parts. . . commonly "body," "mind," and "spirit."*
> *. . . Rather than try to show how these three principal faculties respond to situations as a sum in every character, artists can create characters that represent one of these faculties and show in the story how these powers of the soul relate to one another.*

. . .Harry is clearly in charge. Hermione is the best thinker. Ron is the cheerleader and flag-waver (in his best moments). When they follow Harry's lead in line — Harry, Hermione, and Ron — all goes well. . .

. . .But when the team breaks down and the players don't play their roles. . . things go wrong in the worst way. . .

. . .Good literature. . . lets us see and pattern our-selves after the right alignment of the soul's powers. When our desires are in line with our will, and both will and desires are obedient to directions from the heart or spirit, we are in operation the way we were designed to be. Turn this upside down, though, so that will and spirit answer to the desires. . . and you have a wreck-in-the-making.

— John Granger,
Looking for God in Harry Potter, p. 89-91

I find this analysis interesting, and it is another way the Potter books remind us, without being preachy, of the lessons which religion teaches.

Besides Harry's friends being symbolic, let's look at the idea of friendship. When Harry is feeling blue, he turns to his friends for lifting up. Ron and Hermione form a team, a

More Dinner Table Questions

Harry is normally a good friend to Hermione and Ron, but occasionally, he gets angry or frustrated with them. When does this happen? What makes you upset with your friends? What does Harry do that causes he and Ron to have a big disagreement in *Goblet of Fire*? What do they do to forgive each other and get back to being friends again? Do Harry, Ron, and Hermione make new friends in the books? How do they find new friends?

Harry support group. The two of them seem to know what Harry needs, they help him in his efforts to fight Voldemort, and they bear his frustrations and anger when he takes his problems out on them.

Our Friendships

How do our friendships support us? How do we support our friendships? Do we make sure to see our friends through rough times and rejoice with them in good times? When our friends need information, do we research for them, like Hermione? When our friends need cheerleading, do we root for them like Ron, giving our friends the boost they need to run the race? The race might be having another baby, adopting a child, getting through a move, hanging tough through a temporary period of unemployment, facing a job change, difficulties with neighbors, or issues with the Church.

Do we lead our friends in the right direction, like Harry? Sometimes our best chance of evangelizing isn't in darkest Peru or Hindu India, but right in our own circle of family and friends. Are we brave enough to speak the truth in love?

Difficult circumstances in our lives can tempt us into downheartedness. We don't see Voldemort after us, looking for a fight, as Harry does. We each have our own demons. We may have a tendency to depression, have a tough time with toddlers, wonder how to handle the three teens in the house, have a troublesome in-law, or a distant spouse. Whatever it is, we all go through rough times.

I Want to Be Alone

We have a tendency to push people away during bad times. We throw ourselves a pity party, saying to ourselves, *"If my friends cared, they'd call me. No one is calling. I have no friends."* We think we send out little distress signals. We

think they ought to know we're having a hard time and need them. We hope they can see how poorly we're coping and instinctively *understand* we need a lunch out, a meal delivered, or someone to take the kids for the afternoon.

We wishfully think our friends can read our minds. By waiting for them to call, we're really pushing them away. If we don't allow them into our bad times, they won't be there for us in the good times, either.

A few weeks ago, I was going through such a time. Financial worries, children's health worries, personal health issues, homeschool worries, a car accident, and then, to top it all off, our dryer died. I was low. I didn't answer my e-mail for a few

CHESTERTON

Mahound is in his paradise above the evening star,
(Don John of Austria is going to the war.)
He moves a mighty turban on the timeless houri's
*   knees,*
His turban that is woven of the sunset and the seas.
      — *G.K. Chesterton,* Lepanto, *lines 36-39*

Harry breathed in the funny smell that seemed to come from Quirrell's turban.
      — SS, p. 292

The "timeless houri," the reward or "heaven" in the Mohammedan paradise, is the companionship of beautiful women throughout eternity. A "houri" is a dark-eyed nymph. In an evil twist, Mahound will kill — thus the turban turns red as sunset — for his reward.

Quirrell has entered into a sick friendship, for hidden under his turban lies an ugly secret. When we make friends with evil, the results aren't pleasant.

days, and two of my friends wrote and asked if I was okay. Wallowing in my sadness, I thought they could have at least called me. *What kind of friends are they?* I wondered. *How much do they care?* I didn't want to answer the e-mails because if I didn't, I could add *don't have any friends that really care* to my list of woes, and be justified in feeling lousy.

I was sitting there staring at the computer screen, when a line from Harry Potter went through my head.

Keep your friends close, Harry. . . .

Keep your friends close. I took a deep breath, and realized what I was about to do, in not answering these "What's going on? Haven't heard from you lately," e-mails, was just the opposite: pushing my friends away, not allowing them to enter into my distress and not giving them a chance to cheer me up or help.

What Am I Saying? I Need My Friends!

I sat up straight, and composed letters to each of them, telling them what was going on. They both cheered me up, and I remembered they were friends in good times and in bad, because that's what real friends are. I got out of my slump by allowing my friends to share my burden. I hope I would do the same for them.

Fighting against our natural inclinations is a spiritual battle. Friends can help us. Many of the best saints in the Church had friendships with other saints; St. Rose of Lima and St. Martin de Porres, St. John Bosco and Saint Dominic Savio, and St. Ignatius Loyola and St. Francis Xavier are examples.

> *There is nothing so precious as a faithful friend, and no scales can measure his excellence.*
>
> — Sirach 6:15

The entire sixth chapter of Sirach is about friendship. Friendship is important.

When Harry is trapped in his uncle and aunt's house, unable to even receive mail from his friends, Ron and his twin older brothers come to Harry's rescue. Ron knows his friend wants to escape from the awful circumstances he endures in the home of his relatives, and he responds.

When Harry is believed to be a villain by the entire student body, Ron and Hermione stick up for him, defending him against the others. They remain his faithful friends, and don't desert him.

Harry's aunt and uncle have many material possessions, but have never shown Harry love. And they're miserably unhappy. The entire Weasley family befriends Harry; the family is not wealthy, which causes Ron occasional embarrassment. But they're cheerful, close-knit, and happy. Harry recognizes the Weasley's wealth is a different kind of treasure: family love. What a great message for our children.

The contrast in the Potter books to Harry, Ron, and Hermione is the triplet of Malfoy, Crabbe, and Goyle. Malfoy is a boy in Harry's class whose family has been on the dark side for eons, followers of the evil Lord. Crabbe and Goyle are friends, but serve as bodyguards and the laugh track to Malfoy's mean-spirited remarks. Crabbe and Goyle stick by Malfoy, but their friendship is skewed by the mutual desire for power and position within the Dark Lord's league of followers.

Our Children's Friendships

Good friends strengthen our moral character. In one example from the Potter books, Ron and Hermione have had a falling out and are no longer talking. Harry sides with Ron, and Hermione ends up visiting a mutual friend, Hagrid, and pouring out her troubles to him. In an extraordinary scene, Hagrid invites Harry and Ron to tea, and discusses with

them the importance of friendship: people are more important than their pets and broomsticks. Harry and Ron are remorseful, and consequently make the effort to restore their friendship with Hermione.

Good friends remind us, too, when we are behaving badly. It takes a good friend to let us know when we've stepped over the line, or gone too far in a situation where our emotions have blinded us to what we're doing. Good friends help us on the road to sanctity.

The friendships between the characters in Harry Potter show us what is admirable and helpful about friendship. Hagrid, Harry, Ron, and Hermione have their hearts in the right place. The things they love about each other are not superficial things, but essential traits. Having our hearts in the right place requires seeing our friends as we see ourselves. We want to do for our friends what we would like them to do for us, as the golden rule reminds us. For these reasons, real friendships help us be the saints-in-the-making we're called to be.

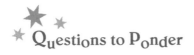

Questions to Ponder

1. Make a list of your friends. Are they real friendships? How do you cultivate your friendships? Have you let any old friendships go you wish you could gain back? What kind of new friend would you like to make?
2. What kinds of things do you wish your friends would do for you? List the traits you think make a good friend. Pick one thing, and work on it so you'll be a good friend to *your* friends.
3. How can you encourage your children's friendships? How do you teach your children to *be* good friends? Do your children have the kind of friends who will help them become virtuous adults?

Up Next

What storybook character was your hero when you were a child? Who is your child's storybook hero? What do you think about heroes? We'll explore the idea of heroes and our children in the next chapter.

Chapter Nine

Harry Potter: Boy Hero

Heroes and Our Children

We start by telling our children stories. Before we ever read the first novel, we tell them about the day mommy and daddy got married, about the day they were born, or about the day the puppy came home to live with us. We tell our children stories about when we were little, stories about their grandparents, and stories about Jesus. Our children's first heroes are their parents, their grandparents, a famous relative or family friend, and Jesus.

After children have heard these stories over and over again, we start reading books to them, and new heroes enter their lives. By then, we've already started forming their imaginations, so if we read a "bad" book together we can still learn from it. As we parents are very careful about what kind of heroes we want our children imitating, we are particular about the books we choose for them. When we read books together, though, we have a far greater ability to influence how our children think about those books.

Parent's Guide to Reviewing Books for Their Children

Toddler — Pre-read books. Time: Less than a minute.
Preschool — Pre-read books. Time: Less than 10 minutes.
Early Elementary — Pre-read books. Time: 20 minutes.
Fourth Grade and up — Book Reviews. Time: 30 minutes.

At the start of our children's book careers, we can keep up pre-reading the books we choose for them to read independently. At some point in their young lives, if they become voracious about reading, they start to outpace us. We switch over to checking book reviews. Finding trustworthy book review sites is a challenge, and most parents use more than one (see Bibliography on page 173).

Book Recommendations You Can Trust

We rely on friends and other trusted adults to point out good and bad books. We may get a bad tip: the book a neighbor recommended for your ten-year-old covers more boy-girl relationship material than your daughter needs to know, in your opinion. You'll get more information next time she mentions a book title to you. A sister-in-law suggests a picture book and next thing you know, it's a family favorite.

Our children need heroes, role models to look up to and model their lives after. They need ideals to strive for, high expectations to live up to. We parents want our children to build character, be morally upright, obtain the virtues, and in every way strive to become living saints: as much as is possible on earth. Our ultimate goal is not the best education, the best college, or landing the highest paying job. Our goal for our family is heaven.

The best role models for our children are parents striving to be saintly themselves. If you're like me, you have a sense of shortcoming in the saint department. A better role model is Jesus. Many children sense though, that Jesus, being God, has left us big sandals to fill. He was not only sinless but also incapable of sinning, unlike the rest of us. That doesn't make him a bad role model; it makes him a perfect role model. But for some children, the ideal of Jesus seems unattainable. These children sometimes prefer the saints as role models.

Saintly Heroes

Saints are just like us: they all need to struggle to resist temptation. They struggle, just as we do, and they win the race. Saints are great role models: heroes for our children. It's good to read lots of stories of the saints to our children, and have them read saint biographies when they are older.

Sometimes, though, as I mentioned in an earlier chapter, children need fictional stories. For some children, it's still hard to read about a saint who begged to receive her First Holy Communion, and when she was allowed to, she died — right there on the spot — kneeling in adoration, as happened to Blessed Imelda Lambertini. It's a wonderful story, but it's a religious story, and some children just don't respond to religious stories.

For those children, parents need to choose non-religious stories with high moral values which extol the virtues, teach the value of good character traits, and help our children see the outcome of various types of behavior. These stories might never mention God, but the power of the story still teaches the morals and values we want to instill in our children. William Bennet's *Book of Virtues* and *Book of Heroes* are filled with such stories.

> *Lord knows, kids. . . need a hero: courageous, self-sacrificing people; setting examples for all of us — everybody loves a hero.*
> — Aunt May, *Spider-Man 2*

Harry the Hero

The Potter series is a typical "hero" story. There are story elements which typify the "hero's journey" such as the call to adventure, crossing the first threshold, initiation, trials, magical flight, etc. Myths are often analyzed revealing typical ways in which the stories progress. A literary analysis shows

that the Harry Potter stories follow these mythical hero journey story lines.

Harry isn't born a hero. He must grow up; he makes mistakes, some serious. His actions have consequences. He isn't perfect, but he's growing in maturity as the books progress. He struggles with his schoolwork; he isn't really good in any one subject, but rather good at sports. He has friends, but not everyone likes him. He's not devastatingly handsome; he has hair that won't lay down straight, is on the thin side, and wears glasses. Children relate to his normalcy.

Harry, Luke, Peter, and Arthur

The Potter story contains many of the same elements as Star Wars, Spider-Man and the Legend of Arthur. Luke Skywalker, Peter Parker and Arthur are very much like Harry; Obi-Wan Kenobi, Uncle Ben/Aunt May and Merlin can be compared to Dumbledore; the Sword in the Stone to the Sword pulled out of the Gryffindor hat — only a true Gryffindor could have pulled that out of the hat, says Dumbledore. Harry, like Arthur, Peter Parker, and Luke Skywalker is an orphan and an only son. Harry and Arthur, after their parents are killed, are taken away by powerful wizards who watch over them from afar.

Each boy has a destiny and a prophecy about him. Harry and Luke both have guardians who know their past, but prefer not to acknowledge the truth. Merlin teaches Arthur wisdom by transforming him into various animals and fish so that Arthur can learn; Harry turns into a fish while competing in the tournament, and can fly both his broomstick and a hippogriff. Arthur's mentor Merlin dies, and Arthur must carry on without him. Harry's mentor dies, and Harry must carry on alone. Arthur forms the Knights of the Round Table, Harry forms Dumbledore's Army.

In each case, the analogy will fall short, in King Arthur, Spider-Man, Star Wars, and Harry Potter; because the only

More Dinner Table Questions

How are Harry and Jesus to be compared? Does Harry teach others? Is he kind and good? Does he welcome strangers? Does he tell stories? Does he save people? How are Harry and Jesus alike, and how are they different?

perfect hero is Jesus. Still, hero stories can teach us about what it means to live our lives.

What kind of hero is Harry? Does Harry really get away with misbehavior? Is he a bad example to our children? Why does he break the rules? Does he disrespect authority?

What about Jesus? Walking along, eating and curing the sick on the Sabbath, not washing ritually? Getting angry in the temple and throwing people out? Was Jesus a rule-breaker, too?

> *"The Sabbath was made for man, not man for the Sabbath," was Jesus' answer to the Pharisees who criticized him for gathering food on a day dedicated to the Lord, and, from the beginning, Christian ethics and moral theology have been inherently casuistic in taking full account of the spiritual condition and intention of the sinner as well as of the circumstances in which the sin was committed.*
>
> — Fleming, p. 12

Harry's ethics and morals are casuistic, or case based, as well. There are times when, as a parent, one wishes Harry would act differently. Harry gives in to his anger and his own emotions to such a point that in one book, his lack of judgment contributes to the death of someone close to him.

Spider-Man, Peter Parker, also a hero who gives in to anger, is in a situation where he isn't paid for the work he did, and gets angry with his "boss." When his boss is robbed, Peter allows the robber to get away, though he could have stopped him. The robber tries to steal a car and when the driver refuses to leave, he's shot. The driver was Parker's uncle. Now Peter must live believing he could have prevented his uncle's death; his behavior, acted out in anger, caused him to believe he shared in the responsibility for his uncle's death.

In both of these cases, although extreme, the story clearly teaches that our actions and inactions have consequences, sometimes permanent consequences. We hope our children will never make a mistake so bad it will cost someone their life. But things happen, and we never know. Perhaps a cautionary tale will help our children think twice before acting in anger.

Rules are important and must be followed. When children are young, the house rules are black and white. If you

---

Oops! We chose a "bad" book.

What happens when you get a book from the library, or open a book as a gift, and you start reading it out loud, and suddenly realize you really don't want your child exposed to whatever it's about? Or they've already read it!

To redeem the situation, all you need to do is talk to your child. Honestly point out what it is that's in the book that doesn't follow your family's moral code. Tell your children truthfully that the world-view, or the morality, or the situational ethics, or whatever it is, that is espoused in the book, is not what your family believes, and explain why. The book may open up a great conversation about a topic that you may not have considered important until now. Use the "bad" book situation as an opportunity to teach your children, and good can come out of it.

don't finish your homework, you don't get to play. But as children mature, they begin to understand that the consequences of rule breaking are varied, just as rules vary in different situations. At our home, there is a rule against swearing and hitting. In a friend's house, there may be no such rules. Our children learn that rules may differ in other places, but that they need to follow our rules even when elsewhere.

In addition to that, pre-teens and especially teens are beginning to learn some rules and laws aren't good and shouldn't be followed. Abortion is legal in our country: that doesn't make it right. Hitler asked for Germans to turn in Jews. That wasn't right. Our country does many things with which we don't agree. We want our children to help fight to fix our country, not become automatons who just follow the rules without thinking.

Harry does normally follow the rules, in fact, when he doesn't he lands in detention. In OP, Harry should have practiced defense against the dreams he was seeing in his head — Dumbledore told him this was his more important job — yet his curiosity led him to continue wanting to see what was just around the corner, in the next open doorway. Voldemort uses Harry's curiosity to trick him into believing someone he loves is in trouble. The situation ends with Harry full of remorse.

Dumbledore sped down the steps past Neville and Harry, who had no more thought of leaving. Dumbledore was already at the foot of the steps when the Death Eaters nearest realized he was there. There were yells; one of the Death Eaters ran for it, scrabbling like a monkey up the stone steps opposite. Dumbledore's spell pulled him back as easily and effortlessly as thought he had hooked him with an invisible line.

— OP, p. 805

CHESTERTON

*St. Michael's on his Mountain in the sea-roads of the
   north
(Don John of Austria is girt and going forth.)
Where the grey seas glitter and the sharp tides shift
And the sea folk labour and the red sails lift.
He shakes his lance of iron and he claps his wings of
   stone. . .*
            — G.K. Chesterton, Lepanto, lines 74-78

*Harry turned to look where Neville was staring.
Directly above them, framed in the doorway from
the Brain Room, stood Albus Dumbledore, his wand
aloft, his face white and furious. Harry felt a kind of
electric charge surge through every particle of his
body* — they were saved.
                                    — OP, p. 805

Mont St. Michael is a rocky islet off the coast of France. Dedicated to St. Michael the Archangel, our patron in battles — spiritual and physical — where the forces of good must overcome the forces of evil. According to Scripture in the book of Revelation, St. Michael fought off Lucifer, Prince of Darkness, and all his angels. Chesterton says the Christians called on St. Michael to help fight the battle against Ali Pasha.

Harry and his friends are losing the battle against the evil Dark Lord and his followers, the Death Eaters. Just when it looks as if all hope is lost, Dumbledore enters, and Harry feels certain the tides of the battle have just turned in their favor.

"Did you catch this man?" asked the colonel, frowning.

Father Brown looked him full in his frowning face. "Yes," he said, "I caught him, with an unseen hook and an invisible line which is long enough to let him wander to the ends of the world, and still bring him back with a twitch upon the thread."

— G.K. Chesterton, "The Queer Feet," in *The Annotated Innocence of Father Brown*, pp. 78-79

Most often, Harry chooses to save a life over following the rules, or prevent an evil, rather than getting in before curfew. Most often, Peter Parker saves lives and prevents destruction as Spider-Man. But they're both human, and like us, make mistakes.

Our children need heroes of all types. If we can choose literature that reflects our values and has the moral consequences we would like our children to learn, a children's story can become more than just a story. It can become a cautionary tale, a story of virtue, goodness, and character building, without ever mentioning religion or God.

Questions to Ponder

1. What values, virtues, and morals should stories reflect that would make them acceptable for your children to read?
2. If a story failed to reflect your values, how could you redeem the situation with your children, after the book has already been read?
3. If you had a discussion with your children about heroes, what would you say about Harry Potter? Who else is a hero in the Potter books?

Up Next

One of the songs I listened to when I was a teen was by Huey Lewis and the News, called "The Power of Love." It had a strong beat and joyfully reported all of the wonderful things love could do in your life. Love plays an important role in the Potter books; let's take a look at the power of love in the next chapter.

Chapter Ten

Harry Potter and the Importance of Love

Why do people have to fight? Fighting seems so barbaric. Yet Chesterton claims that loving something and fighting for it go hand in hand, "the two imply each other," he says. "You cannot love a thing without wanting to fight for it. You cannot fight without something to fight for. To love a thing without wishing to fight for it is not love at all..." says Gilbert Chesterton.

> *A man is sworn to protect his family. He must protect the place of the family, which is the home. When men fight to protect their homes, they fight valiantly and fiercely. When men fight to take another man's home, they fight coldly and cowardly, preying on the weak and destroying what is good only for the sake of destruction...*
> — Dale Ahlquist, *Catholic Men's Quarterly*, Summer/Fall 2006, p. 5

The Power of Love

Jerry L. Walls in "Heaven, Hell, and Harry Potter," in *Harry Potter and Philosophy*, writes:

> *... the nature of ultimate reality, the fundamental metaphysical truth, is loving relationship. God from all eternity has existed as a loving relationship among three persons. Moreover, God loves all His creatures so deeply that He was willing to sacrifice himself to show how*

much He Loves them and wants them to love Him in return. This is what is involved in the Christian belief that Jesus is the Son of God who willingly died for us on the cross to save us from our sins.

If this is true, the story about Harry Potter's mother and the power of her blood is a reflection of one of the deepest truths about reality, namely, that all of us are loved by One who was willing to spill his blood and die for us. Furthermore, the love of Harry's mother is a picture of the fact that love is a greater and more powerful thing than evil and death. It was her sacrificial love that protected Harry when Voldemort/Quirrell tried to kill him. In the Christian story, the resurrection of Jesus shows that love is stronger than death. Jesus offers to share his life with all who believe in him, and this life gives those who receive it the power to live forever. So understood, Christianity is a great love story and it is based on the belief that love is the deepest reality and evil cannot defeat it.

As Dumbledore explains to Harry, the one thing Voldemort cannot understand is love (SS, p. 299). His way of life is the complete opposite of love. Rather than being willing to sacrifice himself for others, he is willing to sacrifice innocent beings for his own selfish purposes.

— "Heaven, Hell, and Harry Potter,"
in *Harry Potter and Philosophy*, p. 74-75

Self-Sacrificial Love

The deepest, most powerful expression of good in the Harry Potter books is the self-sacrificing love which Lily Potter, Harry's mother, showed in protecting her infant son from Lord Voldemort, offering herself as a substitute for her only son's life, and ultimately giving up her life. Her loving

sacrifice is a charm powerful enough to prevent Harry's death as an infant, and this love also saves him in his encounters with Lord Voldemort in school.

Harry and his friends catch the train at King's Cross Station. King's Cross. It's the real name of a station, but the choice points to something Rowling wants to say. The "cross of the king" changes the direction of our lives, too, doesn't it?

Whose Blood Saves Us?

The Blood of the Lamb, the Eucharist, the Blood of Christ saves us. A story where blood saves should seem very familiar to us. The blood of the lamb saved the Israelites from the Angel of Death, ready to kill every first born in Egypt. Christ's blood saves us. Lily's blood saved Harry.

Lily's inoculation of love may also have protected Harry from the very unloving and uncaring environment of his uncle and aunt's home. After 10 years of being ignored, pushed around, and scolded, Harry is still a normal boy, who is neither scarred by his rough treatment, nor bitter about his lack of a loving home.

More Dinner Table Questions

Or maybe this discussion should be after dinner, since we're going to be talking about blood. Compare the Passover, where the blood of the lamb had to be spread over the doorposts; the Last Supper, where Jesus tells his disciples, "This is my blood of the new covenant;" and Harry's mother's blood, Aunt Petunia, and the blood Voldemort takes from Harry. The unicorn is often used as a symbol for Christ, like the white lamb, it is something pure, innocent, and unblemished. Voldemort kills a unicorn and drinks its blood to save his life. What does the blood stand for or signify? Why is blood so important in stories?

In addition, Harry's love for his friends, his adult mentors and guides, and for doing what is right motivates him to fight against Lord Voldemort. Love is stronger than evil and overcomes it in each instance. Even though the evil rises to power and becomes more deadly, love remains the stronger power.

The love theme runs throughout the seven-book series. There is an interesting article about the seven virtues called "Hogwarts, School of Virtue" (see www.osv.com/harrypotter), wherein the author suggests each of the seven books emphasizes a particular virtue. The article is very good and suggests love, though woven through the other books, is the theme of the seventh book.

Love Has at Least 16 Dictionary Meanings

Love takes many forms, although — unfortunately — in English we have but one word for many ideas. We love Harry Potter. We love our parents, we love our country. We love our children, we love our causes. All these "loves" aren't the same.

> *"Greater love has no man than this, that a man lay down his life for his friends."*
> — John 15:13

There are friends in Harry Potter who love each other. Harry, Ron, and Hermione watch out for each other, and I believe would die for each other. Their bond of friendship is quite strong, after having lived through many perils together. Ron and Hermione feel protective of Harry, and try their best to work together to overcome problems, and face things together. In each case, when they work together, they are stronger than if one is alone.

There is physical love in the Harry Potter books. The most fully developed couple is Ron's parents, the Weasleys. They have seven children, whom they love and protect; yet they include Harry and treat him like their own, too. This is magnanimous love, which they have embodied in the generous size of their family. James and Lily Potter, too, married and had Harry; from the wizarding pictures and the mirror of Erised, Harry sees two people loving each other and himself.

Harry's youthfulness prevents him from experiencing this physical kind of love, as it is a mature love which attracts people to each other and then causes them to make vows. Harry's first crush, a girl named Cho Chang, is a cause for inner turmoil in Harry. He neither knows how to act around her, nor does he understand the swooping feeling he experiences in his stomach.

Frequently, I'm asked for advice about Harry Potter problems such as this:

I let my fourteen year old start the Harry Potter series, and I just discovered that my eleven- and nine-year-olds have read the first book, too. I've got two more children who are younger. How do I control the Harry Potter thing with so many different ages in one house?

This is a common problem, and it doesn't just apply to Harry Potter, obviously. If the eleven- and nine-year-olds have already read the first book (and you don't want them to read more), simply explain to them that in your house, these books are for older children, and they may read them when they turn fourteen (or whatever age you set as appropriate for reading the books. Just because a child has read one book, doesn't mean they must read the rest NOW. You are in charge: you make the rules.

CHESTERTON

*The Pope was in his chapel before day or battle
   broke,
(Don John of Austria is hidden in the smoke.)
The hidden room in man's house where God sits all
   the year,
The secret window whence the world looks small
   and very dear.*
      — G.K. Chesterton, Lepanto, lines 108-111

*"I cared about you too much," said Dumbledore
simply. "I cared more for your happiness than your
knowing the truth, more for your peace of mind than
my plan, more for your life than the lives that might
be lost if the plan failed. In other words, I acted
exactly as Voldemort expects we fools who love to
act."*
                                                    — OP, p. 838

The Pope was praying in his chapel. The hidden room is the
tabernacle, with the Blessed Sacrament inside, hiding from
the world. The Pope cared so much about the battle of Lepanto, he spent the day in his chapel praying for Don John
and his troops. Although fighting a battle was not what he
had planned, the Pope felt he had to help defend Europe
from an invading army bent on the despoliation, destruction,
and hostile takeover of land not theirs. The Christians were
on the defense, outnumbered, outmaneuvered, with inexpe-
rienced leadership, and even the wind against them; the
Pope pleaded for help from heaven, since from an earthly
point of view, it was hopeless.

Dumbledore must explain the whole outline of his plan to save Harry from the pain of having to fight Voldemort. Dumbledore understood with his mind what needed to be done, but acted with his heart, his emotions, to prevent someone he loved from being hurt. His mistake cost a life, and Dumbledore is sorry. He now tells Harry what he needs to know to win the battle.

Harry's second love interest, Ginny Weasley, is his best friend's younger sister. It's very sweet to read about Harry wondering whether Ginny is someone he should pursue, knowing she's Ron's sister. Harry figures out he and Ginny have much in common and could be a couple, but he sacrifices their relationship because of his responsibility to vanquish the Dark Lord. He doesn't want to put Ginny in danger, a mature, selfless decision.

Whenever Harry is faced with a decision, he always chooses others over his own needs, wants, and desires. He develops a deep understanding of himself, of self-sacrificing love, of what tasks he must accomplish, what is expected of him, and what love means.

As the father has loved me, so have I loved you; abide in my love. If you keep my commandments, you will abide in my love, just as I have kept my Father's commandments and abide in his love.

— John 15: 9-10

When Harry and his mentor, Professor Dumbledore, go on a dangerous journey, they both know there may be trouble. First, Dumbledore makes Harry swear obedience: he must do whatever Dumbledore asks him, no questions asked. Harry promises. When Ron and Hermione question

Harry about going with Dumbledore, Harry expresses his complete trust in Dumbledore by stating, "I'll be fine, I'll be with Dumbledore." After a night's adventure, they return, Dumbledore injured, Harry assisting him. When Harry encourages his Headmaster, saying, "We're nearly there, don't worry," Dumbledore pays him the compliment of saying, "I'm not worried, Harry, I am with you."

The mutual trust between teacher and student, between mentor and youth is visible here in this dialog. Harry must obey and trust Dumbledore, but Dumbledore states that he trusts Harry.

God Trusts Us

Thinking about this led me to wonder how we sometimes forget that although we should place our complete trust in God and give him our total obedience, God trusts us, too. He gives us free will and allows us to make our own choices. But he trusts us to make the right decisions. That's why our sin damages our relationship with God, he's sad; he trusted us.

And Jesus trusted his disciples to carry on his work, and in the same sense, he trusts us today to *keep* carrying on his work. If we aren't doing his work in the world today, who is? Peter, Paul, James, and John are long dead. We have to be the hands and feet of Christ, he trusts us.

Harry loves his friends and family, he loves the school he attends, and he loves the Headmaster. Harry loves the Order of the Phoenix and his Quidditch team. At some point, Harry must decide what to fight for. He loves and cherishes his parents, he knows the Order of the Phoenix is fighting for truth and goodness, and he chooses to join them against the bad guys. Harry fights the Evil Lord because Voldemort killed his parents, but he isn't seeking revenge. His parents are dead, and there's nothing he can do about it. He wants to fight Voldemort because the Dark Lord is destructive; he murders for no reason, he creates friction

and discord, he causes destruction wherever he goes. Harry wants to fight Voldemort because he wants to protect the things and people he loves.

> *The true soldier fights not because he hates what is in front of him, but because he loves what is behind him.*
> — G.K. Chesterton, ILN, 1/14/11

If there is one overarching theme in the Harry Potter books, it is love conquers all; a good message for our children. And the best love of all is the self-sacrificial love, the love ready to lay down its life for another.

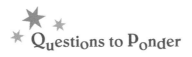

Questions to Ponder

1. How can we best teach our children that love is more than our society says it is: a warm good feeling? How do we teach them that love is a decision? How do we teach them self-sacrificing love?
2. How can we sacrifice enough for our children to learn about self-sacrifice, but not enough so that they take advantage of our generosity? Should we put limits on our love?
3. What do you love enough to fight for to the end? How do our children learn what they should defend?
4. What does God teach us about Love? What does Jesus? How did we learn about love? What is the best example of love in Scripture?

> *Love bears all things, believes all things, hopes all things, endures all things.*
> — 1 Corinthians 13:7

Up Next

What difference does it make if you are a teen or an adult reading the Potter books? The books are the same either way, aren't they? We'll look at ways people read the books in the next chapter.

Chapter Eleven

Finding Ourselves in Harry Potter

Am I a Part of the Story?

A book such as Harry Potter succeeds if readers can relate to the hero, if they can see themselves in the characters, if they feel a part of the story. Harry Potter is not a saint. He makes mistakes, he gets angry, he has fights with his friends, and they make up. If Harry were only a wizard doing magic tricks, no child could ever relate to him. The Harry Potter books succeed because we can see ourselves in Harry, making mistakes, sinning at times, but coming through with courage when the situation demands it.

When Scholastic ran a competition asking children to tell, "How the Harry Potter Books Changed My Life," the essays explained how one of the book's three main characters helped them to cope with illness, abuse, bullying, or poor self-esteem. Children see their own situations in Harry

More Dinner Table Questions

Ask your children to tell you how the Harry Potter books have changed their lives. Do they try harder to be brave? Are they a better friend? Do they try to do what's right instead of what's easy (and wrong)? Do the books help them deal with bullies? Or have they simply been entertained? For some younger children, the level of understanding the deeper meanings in Harry Potter might not be there yet. But with your help, perhaps you'll help your children see that there are things in Harry Potter that they can apply to their own lives.

Potter — even if vastly different from the book — because the books deal with people and their feelings.

When I first began to do some research into the Harry Potter phenomenon, I came across John Granger's book, *Looking for God in Harry Potter*. Just seeing the title, I thought, *I don't want to find God in Harry Potter; I want to find myself.* Later, Mr. Granger confessed he didn't pick it, or think it was the best title.

What was I looking for? In my ever-present quest for practical spiritual guidance, I normally read non-fiction with titles such as *Handling the Cooking and Laundry Like the Saints*, or *Life on a Budget: Let Jesus Be Your Financial Counselor*, or *How Reading Church Encyclicals Radically Changed My Life*. I look for ideas to conquer temptations, gain patience and wisdom, and learn how to handle anger and selfishness while doing my normal everyday duties. If I can gain one nugget from a book, it's worth reading.

Based on my experience, I know the Harry Potter books are full of ideas that cause one to pause and think. In this way, they remind me of G.K. Chesterton's books, although Rowling's are much easier to read. Chesterton's work is so packed with ideas, that one reads a line or two, and then must pause and wonder about what was just said. Chesterton has a way of writing that makes flashes go off in the brain. The reader is stunned by the upside-down world presented by Chesterton, that looks so right-side-up.

Rowling's books work in a completely different way, but the outcome is the same. In a novel that is compelling and easy for an adult or child to read, she packs ideas and themes which invite the reader into deeper thinking: death, choices, love, friendship, temptations, dealing with anger, facing evil, learning from wiser teachers.

Besides thinking about these themes, I think the people who gain the most from reading Rowling's books are those that find themselves in the books. If one sees the scared school girl or boy one once was, if one gets angry and regrets

More Dinner Table Questions

In the later books, Harry spends a lot of time being angry. Sometimes he throws things around, even breaking Dumbledore's property. Discuss this with your children, and see what appropriate ways there are to handle anger. Being angry is a normal feeling. How we act upon our anger is under our control and requires the exercise of free will.

what one says, if one pushes away friends and then realizes it's a mistake, if one experiences the death of a loved one — these are universal experiences, and Rowling is wonderful at describing how her characters feel because she's felt as we've all felt, and we see ourselves in her stories.

Dealing with Death

When Rowling was still a very young adult, she lost her mother to multiple sclerosis. Her mother had been ill since Rowling was a teen, and this affected how she felt about life. Writing helped her deal with the death.

Although evil is present all around us, our society is timid about calling something evil. Yet, we know that when an innocent five-year-old girl is hit by the bullet of a passing gang member randomly shooting in windows, paralyzing her for life, or when an innocent young woman is riding her bike along a winding parkway on a summer afternoon and is taken, defiled, and murdered just for being in the wrong place at the wrong time, we recognize evil.

The Love of a Mother

Although I saw myself in the Harry character, the person I could most relate to in the Rowling books is Mrs. Weasley.

Molly is a tender-hearted mother hen, caring for her children in the normal ways: doing their laundry, folding their socks, making meals, and doing the dishes. When Harry needs a place to stay, she takes him in and helps him buy his school books. She hugs and kisses her children, worries about them, and loves them unconditionally. She is a great example of hospitality, warmth, openness to life, and of loving. She and her husband Arthur have a loving and close relationship. They work and live together in harmony. Molly is a great example to me.

> *And even in order that the novelist should kill people, it is first necessary that he should make them live.*
> — G.K. Chesterton

Adults vs. Children Reading Harry Potter

For children, especially those who have been following Harry Potter along as a series, the books are often read quickly, absorbed quickly, and the ending is very important. A teenaged girl I know reads the endings first, to reassure herself that things go right. A nephew had the statistics on each book: he's read three of them in one day, and the others in less than 24 hours. He's not reading them to gain a deep understanding of the story; he wants the plot line and the ending. Then, he's done. He hasn't re-read them.

Some children I know are on their third and fourth reading of the series. In order to want to read *that* many pages a second, third, or fourth time, there has to be something interesting there. Because the stories are mysteries, after you've read them once, you know "who-done-it" — why would a child read them another time?

I've discovered in reading the books that Rowling has a great sense of humor, and she's hidden humorous wordings, names, places, and things that the reader might overlook

CHESTERTON

He sees as in a mirror on the monstrous twilight sea
The crescent of his cruel ships whose name is
*   mystery;*

> — Chesterton, Lepanto, lines 112-113

For now we see in a mirror dimly, but then face to
face. Now I know in part; then I shall understand
fully, even as I have been fully understood.

> — 1 Corinthians 13:12

"It only put me in Gryffindor," said Harry in a defeated
voice, "Because I asked not to go in Slytherin. . . ."

*   "Exactly," said Dumbledore, beaming once*
more. "Which makes you *very different from Tom*
Riddle. It is our choices, Harry, that show what we
truly are, far more than our abilities." Harry sat
motionless in his chair, stunned.

> — *CS,* p. 333

The Pope had a vision of the battle during his prayer, and was aware of the turn of the tide for victory. The odds were against the troops, the chances of winning slim, if they were on their own. But due to the action of the Pope, and the prayers of many, they were victorious. No one had to pray that day. The Pope could have gone about his business, hoping that God would take care of the situation if he chose to in His own way. But the Pope *chose* to pray. He *chose* to ask others to pray. We all make choices every day.

Harry has certain skills and talents. He could use them for good, or to gain personal power. Harry wants the good, and chooses the good. He actively engages his will to change the course of his future.

when reading the book quickly the first time, trying to get to the climax. Rowling has managed to create literary works that are both page-turners and word-savoring. This is an ideal mix for book lovers of all types.

Reading for Clues

In addition, when reading the later books, the reader realizes important clues can be found in earlier books. When I began reading the Potter books, there were six of them already published. I read through one after the other until I finished the sixth book. As soon as I put that book down, I immediately felt a desire to read the first few books again. I had missed clues I should have been able to see to uncover the mystery, and I wanted to try again to find the evidence, now that I knew more information. I began to read through the set again.

If an adult is reading the books to himself, he can read through them quickly. However, if an adult is reading the books to a child, he cannot. Reading the books bit by bit to children allows the reader and listeners time to reflect on and discuss what's happening in the books. The adult may read a chapter a day, and then have the whole next day to ponder the meaning of the different events and such in that chapter. This way of reading Harry Potter has produced adults who find deeper meaning in the books. I find it quite interesting that of the three books by Christians about Harry Potter, *Looking for God in Harry Potter, A Charmed Life,* and *The Mystery of Harry Potter,* each of us began our adventures into the world of Harry Potter by hearing the work read out loud. John Granger and I began by reading the books to our children. Francis Bridger was a volunteer in a classroom where his task was to listen to young readers read to him; and what they wanted to read was Harry Potter.

I think this is important. The Potter books require thought to work out what they are all about. J.K. Rowling has said in interviews that she's written the books so that they might not be fully understood on the first reading. Those who don't take the time to discover the depths of the Rowling books won't know the joy of discovery.

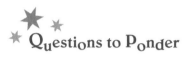

Questions to Ponder

1. How are you like Harry Potter? Or do you see yourself in one of the other of Rowling's characters?
2. If you've read the Potter books, how is your understanding of the books different from your children's?
3. What mistakes does Harry make that you can relate to? What are Harry's strengths? Can you imitate those in your daily life?

Up Next

The Harry Potter movies: To some people, Harry Potter *is* the movies. They haven't read the books and don't plan to. If you only watch the movies, do you really know what the books are about? What role does the author have in the making of the movies? We'll look at the books vs. the movies in the next chapter.

Chapter Twelve

Harry "The Franchise" Potter

What About the Movies?

The movies are not the books. I've mainly discussed the books here, not the movies, video games and other incidental products. I'm not writing about Harry "The Franchise" Potter, I'm writing about Harry "The Books" Potter. Our family loves to watch good movies, but we believe books and stories hold a higher place than movies in the formation of our children's imaginations.

However, the movies are often what people think of when they hear the name Harry Potter, so we'll talk about them a little bit.

Cut to the Chase

Some critics claim the movies are better than the books because they distill all of the action down into the most action-packed moments. Much is lost during the translation onto the big screen, and it is my opinion the movies don't tell the moral story the way it unfolds in the books.

The second problem with the movies is that they really are for older pre-teens and teens. The last two movies have come with PG-13 ratings for sequences of violence and frightening images, so these are hardly children's movies. As mentioned previously, the toys and products associated with these movies are geared for four- to nine-year-olds, making the whole marketing plan problematic for parents. A parent must show extraordinary toughness in telling the young people in the house that they will have to wait till

they're older to see the movies — if they are going to see the movies at all. This is especially difficult when there are some in the house mature enough to see them, and others who aren't. However, this issue isn't exclusive to movies, parents of multi-age children must deal with this all the time.

The general rule in our house is that before we watch a movie, we read the book. We find that often, watching the movie first takes the fun out of reading the book, because the plot and the outcome are already known, if they were true to the book's storyline, that is. Most often, the movies must condense so much that a tremendous amount of the story is left out.

One of the reasons for this is that the author of the books, once she's signed away the rights so that the movie can be made, is out of the loop during the making of the movie. Rowling requested that the movies keep to the books, but that's a request that the filmmakers may or may not take into consideration when writing the script.

Changing Scripts

One thing I dislike in the movies is changed dialogue. For example, I believe that the theme of Harry as hero is important. Our culture is anti-hero, despite popular movies, from *The Incredibles* to *Spider-Man* to *Harry Potter* to *The Return of Superman* to *Star Wars* which all reflect our inner longing for heroes. It just isn't politically correct to talk positively about heroes.

So the movie scriptwriter pens this conversation in *Harry Potter and the Goblet of Fire*:

> Barty Crouch, Jr.: *"You know what this means, don't you? He's back. Lord Voldemort has returned."*

> Harry (to Dumbledore): *"I'm sorry sir, I couldn't help it."*

Dumbledore (to Professor McGonagall): *"Send an owl to Azkaban. I think they'll find they're missing a prisoner."*

Barty: *"I'll be welcomed back like a hero."*

Dumbledore: *"Perhaps. Personally I've never had much time for heroes."*

I think that's a terrible line, giving lip service to our modern culture. Here's the scene in the book:

Moody who is Barty Crouch, Jr., in disguise, says, "The Dark Lord has returned, with me at his side. . . My master's plan worked. He is returned to power and I will be honored by him beyond the dreams of wizards." An insane smile lit his features and his head dropped onto his shoulder. Nobody speaks. He doesn't say anything about being a hero and neither does Dumbledore reject heroes.

And the entire dialog I mentioned on pages 48-49, where Harry is attempting to discover what lies "beyond the veil," a part of the story of *The Order of the Phoenix* I consider very important, is completely left out of the OOP movie.

Another example: Harry must rescue a loved one in the underwater challenge during the TriWizard Tournament. In the book, he tries to rescue his friend Hermione first before his friend Ron, which is the gentlemanly thing to do. In the movie, they have him rescuing Ron first, and then trying for

---

More Dinner Table Questions

What do you think Dumbledore really thinks about heroes? Who is Dumbledore's hero? Are people heroic because they want to be, or is it just chance? Do some people pretend to be heroes? Can a bad guy, or a villain be a hero?

CHESTERTON

Scarlet running over on the silvers and the golds,
Breaking of the hatches up and bursting of the holds,
Thronging of the thousands up that labour under sea
White for bliss and blind for sun and stunned for
    liberty.
Vivat Hispania!
Domino Gloria!
Don John of Austria
Has set his people free!
    — *G.K. Chesterton, Lepanto, lines 130-137*

"*Hasn't your experience with the Time-Turner taught you anything, Harry? The consequences of our actions are always so complicated, so diverse, that predicting the future is a very difficult business indeed...*"

    — *PA, p. 426*

The "silvers and the golds" hint at the fact that Ali Pasha, admiral of the Turkish ships, had brought along his personal wealth rather than risk having it confiscated should anything happen and he displease his Sultan. The estimate is 150,000 gold sequins. Beneath the ship of the Turks, hidden in the dark below was another kind of gold: previously captured Christian slaves, working the oars for the Turks. When the Christians became the victors, an estimated 12,000 Christian "galley slaves" were set free, blinded by the sunlight. 2000 of the slaves were Spanish, and joined in the cry, "Long Live Spain!" — *Vivat Hispania!*

    No one can predict the future, and we really can't know the consequences of our actions, how they will affect others, and the chain of events they will bring about. Harry has a

chance to free an innocent man, and, due to his actions, the consequences lead to freedom. He acts with courage and trust, not knowing if the end will work out right.

Hermione. It's just a small thing, but the Harry of the books is a nobler person, a person with greater character than the Harry of the movies.

Movie Commentary

If you decide you might want to let your family watch the movies, I suggest that you watch first, to see exactly what kind of "violence and frightening images" there are. You know your children, and will know if they could handle what you've seen. If you decide to let them watch the movies, watch them together. Carry on a bit of a dialog during the movie. You can easily say, "Hey! That wasn't like that in the book. Why do you think the movie makers changed that scene or that dialog?" or "Wow, that's not how I pictured the Dark Lord, how about you?"

I feel certain that the age limits for the books will be lower than the age limits for the movies. Reading a book together with a young child can be comforting. The child is safe and the images of the characters and the action are what he forms in his own mind. Depending on what he's seen in his lifetime, he can be scared by what he thinks of, but he knows, with you by his side, that the story will work out, and the hero will save the day.

With the movies, the intensity of the action is quite physical; a child sees scenes and characters as the moviemakers intend for us to see them, and not as our imaginations allow us to see them. This is the limitation of movies over books, and why books are so much better for

children. Since the movie scenes can be so intense, the child needs to be more mature to handle them.

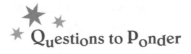

Questions to Ponder

1. Have you or your children seen the Potter movies? What was your initial reaction to them? Why or why not see the movies?
2. If you've seen the movies first without reading the books, would you like to try reading the books together with your children now?
3. If you've read the books and seen the movies, how about trying a contest with your children to point out all the places where the movies are wrong or different from the books? Talk to your children about why the scriptwriters might have wanted to change certain things in the movies. Are there any movie lines or scenes that are better than the book?

It takes a great deal of courage to stand up to your enemies, but a great deal more to stand up to your friends.
— Dumbledore in the *Sorcerer's Stone* Movie

Up Next

Book Seven, *Harry Potter and the Deathly Hallows*, concludes the series. Some people have been reserving their judgment until the end. Will Harry Potter remain consistent as a moral tale, right to the end? Let's discuss this more in the next chapter.

Conclusion

Harry Potter and the Last Word

Book Seven: Harry Potter and the Deathly Hallows

As I finish writing this book, the seventh and final Harry Potter book, *Harry Potter and the Deathly Hallows*, is about to be published. I had originally planned to read the final Harry Potter book before finishing *The Mystery of Harry Potter* so I could ensure the series ended as I have been hoping it will — as a Christian morality tale — and incorporate that into this book. My publisher, however, felt that the basic content of this book was important to get out in advance of the next Harry Potter movie and the final book so that people could already have it in hand when the issues are brought to the forefront once again.

To help you in your analysis of the seventh book, my reflections on it will be posted as a chapter on the publisher's website, www.osv.com/harrypotter, about a week after it is released.

For now, I offer the following reflections:

> *The author cannot tell us until the last chapter any of the most interesting things about the most interesting people. It is a masquerade ball in which everybody is disguised as somebody else, and there is no true personal interest until the clock strikes twelve. That is, as I have said, we cannot really get at the psychology and philosophy, the morals and the religion, of the thing until we have read the last chapter.*
>
> — G.K. Chesterton, *Generally Speaking*, p. 5-6

As Chesterton so rightly says, we couldn't know the outcome of Rowling's work until the last chapter, the seventh book, is written. Until then, it was right for many to withhold judgment. After all, this series is written as a septology: the entire seven books make up one long but continuous story, with the story lines continuing throughout the series, and some facts and faces are hidden behind masks, as Chesterton says, until the last chapter of the last book. Certainly Snape's identity has been kept from us throughout the entire series. Good guy? Bad guy? Haven't we been kept guessing this whole time?

And so although there have been hints, both in the stories themselves, and in interviews with J.K. Rowling, hints enough for us to know that the end of the story would be consistent with the rest of it, some people have judged the books unworthy, though they couldn't know the ending. This judgment, it seems to me, was based on partial information and superficial literary devices used in the stories to tell the deeper story.

Others have preferred to withhold judgment, and see what the seventh book would bring.

Still others joined in the ranks of series supporters, based on those hints in both the stories and the interviews with the author, not knowing what the "last chapter" would be. I have believed, since discovering Harry Potter, that Rowl-

More Dinner Table Questions

What do you hope is in book seven?
What do you think will happen in the end?
How would you write a satisfying ending to the Harry Potter series if you could write it?

ing is a very clever person, who is able to overcome the difficulties of writing a very long detective novel, and that she has been a success at doing it, and so I was willing to jump on the Harry Potter bandwagon before the last chapter.

The End of the Story

Harry Potter is a story. If the Harry Potter story points to the One True Story, and I believe it does in many ways, then it is a good story, and a real story. Like those who heard Jesus' parables, we have hearts that like to hear stories. We hear them, and we know just like Jesus' parables, there are two meanings. And we are, like the disciples, trying to pull Jesus aside.

> *And his disciples came to him, saying, "Explain to us the parable of the weeds of the field."*
> — Matthew 13:36

And Jesus did explain. And we want to pull J.K. Rowling aside and ask her the same question, "Explain what you mean by the story of Harry Potter." But perhaps, as Regina Doman suggests (see interview in Appendix A), she won't tell, so we are kept guessing, and more people will enter into the fairy tale. Jesus didn't explain the parables to *everyone*. While we wait to see if Rowling explains, we discuss Harry Potter among ourselves, and see if we can't figure it out, and hope we are on the right track.

The most important thing we parents can do to help our children understand Harry Potter is to read the books together. Make comments along the way. "Trying to predict the future is impossible, isn't it honey?" or "Wasn't that brave of her to say that when she knew she could get in trouble? Sometimes doing the right thing takes courage, doesn't it?" and so forth. Use the topics that come up as

opportunities to teach. Your children will think of things to ask you, and you will think of things to discuss. Talking with our children about the topics in Harry Potter will be a good thing for the family.

At the end of Chesterton's poem Lepanto, the Christians have had a miraculous victory over the Turks, preventing them again, temporarily, from continuing their ongoing campaign of thievery and malice against Christendom. But the evil still lurks, and will soon want revenge, and the battle is never really over.

Our lives, too, are daily battles. We fight one foe, only to find another waiting in the wings once we think we have everything handled. We are never really done fighting. We may vanquish one enemy, only to find another one tomorrow. But each day, we must take up our crosses and fight. Each day, we must struggle on because the goal is heaven, and it isn't the easy way, but it is the right way.

Morality: Black and White or Casuistry?

If arbitrary statements of right and wrong are no use, if statements concerning justice and wrong are only palaver, how in the world can we be certain that the incidents which happen are injustices? If we have no standard for judging whether anything is right, how on earth can we decide that the world is wrong?

— G.K. Chesterton, ILN, 5/1/26

In the beginning of this book, I told you that one of the reasons I liked Harry Potter was the clear delineation between good and evil. However, then, in order to explain why Harry and his friends sometimes break the rules, I needed to talk about casuistry: the ethical method of taking the circumstances of the situation into consideration, or,

as Dale Ahlquist put it in his interview (see Appendix A), see the windows in the wall that is the rule.

There are stages of moral development. When the baby is young, we tell him "Don't touch the stove!" We don't explain the difference between a stove that's on and a stove that's off, or a stove that might be hot and cause injury and a stove that won't. We have to have a clear, black and white morality: you can either do something, or you can't. The baby, toddler, or pre-school-aged child can't understand that there are circumstances that might change; he must be trained not to touch the stove at all — anytime.

As the child grows and matures, however, we can teach him that there are times when the rules, though absolute and good rules, must be made flexible. When we inform our children that all adults must be respected and obeyed, we are assuming that those adults are worthy of our children's respect, and are issuing orders which we would want our children to obey. If a teacher or coach tells a child to lie, steal, or cheat, naturally, we then must be glad when our child disobeys that adult. These kinds of nuances are for the more mature mind.

There are times, however, when there is danger present, or an action needs an immediate response. Then, once again, we are back to our black and white, good vs. evil type of decision. We must have an interior sense of right and wrong in order to make these snap or quick decisions. Our early moral formation assists us in this task.

So there is a time and place for "black and white" morality, and a time and place for casuistry. Reading Harry Potter in your home, for example, is an example of casuistry. It isn't right — or wrong — for everyone. But the child and family circumstances need to be taken into consideration. Is there a solid moral foundation in the home? Are the parents willing to explain the story? Does the child have an interest in witchcraft? Is the child attracted to "bad"

CHESTERTON

Thronging of the thousands up that labour under sea
White for bliss and blind for sun and stunned for
*   liberty.*
— G.K. Chesterton, Lepanto, lines 132-133

The Battle of Lepanto only lasted one day, but the results were surprising.

The Turks had more seamen, better preparation, more ships, and more oarsmen working below decks. Don John was an unexpected hero. Harry's battle with Voldemort has lasted 17 years, but each time they've met in battle, Harry has unexpectedly defeated the bigger, the more mature, and the better-prepared enemy. With Lepanto, we can say God was on their side. With Harry Potter, we can say goodness was on their side.

characters rather than finding the "good" qualities of the hero attractive?

Good vs. evil, light vs. darkness, right vs. wrong, these are fundamental choices that we will all make.

Finding Symbolism in Harry Potter

I will not reveal what *you* should find in the text of Harry Potter. I had great joy in discovering things there for myself, and I want you to share in that joy. I only hope that by encouraging you to read Harry Potter for yourself, and by telling you there are great things in the books, you might feel a bit like a detective, and want to discover the mystery. Harry Potter is not a spiritual guidebook. There are very

good books that better fit that description, such as: *Introduction to the Devout Life*, *The Imitation of Christ*, *The Story of a Soul*, etc. Harry Potter is not like them. It is a story, and because it reflects all true stories, some parts will ring true. Even if it is a pagan story, even if it is a fairy tale, even if it is a myth or a fantasy, there are still truths in it to be discovered, and no reason why you can't discover them. I hope you and your family have a wonderful time sleuthing and making your own discoveries in J.K. Rowling's books about Harry Potter.

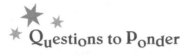

Questions to Ponder

1. One character in particular, Snape, has been mysteriously hidden from us during the first six books. Where do you think his loyalties ultimately lie?
2. How will the mystery of Harry Potter work out in the end?
3. The seventh book will attempt to answer everything mysterious that's left to answer. What questions do you have that you want the seventh book to answer?

Acknowledgments

Thanks to some special people who helped this book along. Maureen Wittmann is an endless font of encouragement, a friend, proofreader, and it was her idea first I write this book. Peter Floriani encouraged me and improved every aspect of this book; and Father Pierre Ingram, C.C. prayed for me and for this book, and let me bounce ideas off him. This is a far better book because of these people. Peter Floriani, Maureen Wittmann, Sean Dailey, Father Pierre, and Jean Taylor were my proofreaders.

Thanks to Dale Ahlquist, Stratford Caldecott, Regina Doman, John Granger, and Mark Shea.

Thanks to the Antioch Public Library District, for helping me with library loans.

Most of all, I'd like to thank Mike, Sarah and Robin. The girls thought their mom had gone mental; after all, what normal adult is *that* into Harry Potter? Thanks for being patient with me through my "Harry" phase.

Appendix A

Interviews

Dale Ahlquist is the President of the American Chesterton Society, and a convert to the Catholic faith. He and his wife Laura have six children. Ahlquist's talks on Chesterton have delighted audiences around the country and the world. Ahlquist is the author of *G.K. Chesterton — The Apostle of Common Sense* and *Common Sense 101: Lessons from G.K. Chesterton*. He is creator and host of the popular "Apostle of Common Sense" television series on EWTN. As a Catholic convert and a Chestertonian, Dale has a unique view on the Harry Potter controversy.

Nancy C. Brown (NCB): Dale, do you let your children read Harry Potter, and if so, how did that come about? Were you ever against the series?

Dale Ahlquist (DA): I don't remember ever being against the series. I read the first books at the same time my oldest two children read them. They were in their mid-teens when they started, and it seems to me that we became aware of the controversy after we had already started reading the books. None of us could imagine why they were controversial. My wife has read all the books as well. We have had very enjoyable and probing family discussions about them. My ten-year-old has now read the first four books. And he read them in one year. The experience turned him into a reader, which he wasn't before.

NCB: How do you Dale, as a Chestertonian, answer the frequent criticism of the Harry Potter books that it is a

"portal" or an introduction into the world of witchcraft and the occult?

Witches and Pirates

DA: The Harry Potter novels simply aren't what the critics say they are. They're well worth reading. They're just as good as the fantasy fiction of J.R.R. Tolkien, C.S. Lewis, and Charles Williams. As good, in fact, as Charles Dickens.

The books are no more a glorification of witchcraft than Robert Louis Stevenson's novels are a glorification of piracy. Yes, we're right to condemn witchcraft and piracy, but children will still be right to play dress up as witches and pirates. It doesn't mean they have an unconscious desire for real warts on their noses and genuinely empty sockets behind their eye patches. Their make-believe of casting spells and mixing potions and swinging swords and hunting for buried loot isn't a sign of degeneracy or a precursor that they're destined for séances and street fights. It's play. Children know the difference. They know something we have forgotten: that heaven, as Chesterton says, is a playground and earth a task garden.

NCB: Why is there witchcraft in Harry Potter then?

DA: I think the witchcraft in the Potter books is merely a vehicle to tell a tale, a tale with clear morals. This is so obvious that even intelligent people can figure it out. The "dark arts" in the books are obviously evil, and the main characters are even taught to defend themselves against such evil, to resist it, not to be lured into it. Good is clearly good, even when it's "good magic." Bad is clearly bad, especially the bad magic. It's the same as in any fairy tale. The fairy godmother's use of magic is good when used to turn the pumpkin into a coach to transport Cinderella to the ball. Let me get Chesterton to explain why fairy tales are good:

Fairy tales are the only true accounts that man has ever given of his destiny. "Jack the Giant-Killer" is the

embodiment of the first of the three great paradoxes by which men live. It is the paradox of Courage: the paradox which says, "You must defy the thing that is terrifying; unless you are frightened, you are not brave." "Cinderella" is the embodiment of the second of the paradoxes by which men live: the paradox of Humility which says "Look for the best in the thing, ignorant of its merit; he that abases himself shall be exalted." And "Beauty and the Beast" is the embodiment of the third of the paradoxes by which men live: the paradox of Faith – the absolutely necessary and wildly unreasonable maxim which says to every mother with a child or to every patriot with a country, "You must love the thing first and make it lovable afterwards."

— *The World*, Sept. 7, 1904)

NCB: So the Potter books are fairy tales then?

DA: I believe they are fairy tales, though they're also something more. All three of Chesterton's paradoxes, the paradox of courage, humility, and faith, are present in the Harry Potter books. Harry is brave. He is terrified at the prospect of defying a large and looming evil. And let's not forget that he doesn't defy what's good — which is what

More Dinner Table Questions

Your family may have friends who don't read Harry Potter. Talk to your children about different families, who have different rules about what can be read and what can't; and how you will not judge other families by whether they read Harry Potter or not. You might also encourage your children to discuss Harry Potter more with you and less with their friends, who may or may not have the Christian moral foundation that your family has.

happens in most modern literature. Harry is humble. He's never overly confident in his own abilities. He's got no tolerance for fame. He counts others as better than himself. And Harry is faithful and charitable.

NCB: Just before, you were saying that Cinderella's fairy godmother used magic for a good cause when she turned the pumpkin into a coach. Critics of the Potter books say that all use of magic is evil. And magic is condemned by the *Catechism*, whereas piracy is, literally, not. How do you answer them?

DA: If the source of the magic is evil spirits, of course there is no difference if the magic is good — which is called "white magic" — or bad — which is called "black magic." But the Potter books are not an endorsement of "white" magic. Neither is Cinderella. And most children know the difference. I'm not as convinced about most adults.

NCB: One of the criticisms of the Potter books is that they interest children in the occult, which we parents naturally don't want. I've also heard that the Potter books have increased our whole society's interest in the occult.

Interest in Witchcraft Up: So Is Interest in Greed, Pride, and Selfishness

DA: A normal child, with normal parents who watch what he reads and talk to him about it, is not going to secretly practice real "dark arts" in his bedroom. To say that there has been an increased interest in the occult as the result of the Harry Potter phenomenon is unfair. There has been an increased interest in the occult for the last thirty years. And also in the last one hundred years. And in the last one thousand years. I've seen a great increase in greed over the same period. And pride and selfishness and all the other much more subtle devices of the devil which have drawn people toward hell. But yes, certainly there has been an increase in the occult. Chesterton noticed it, too, at the beginning of the previous century. In reference to a famous

Gospel story he says that modern thought has left out the Savior and kept the devils and the swine.

NCB: Well, Harry Potter certainly has its devils and swine, but it also, it seems to me, has its savior. Let me ask you another question, this time about Chesterton's youth. Chesterton dabbled in "spiritualism" and did some ouija board experimentation, didn't he?

DA: Yes.

NCB: If someone as brilliantly intellectual as Chesterton could be led astray by the occult, and come back out of it, can't people survive it as an episode in their life, get over it, like Chesterton? I don't mean it's a good thing to get into the occult, I'm just saying, you can break free of it.

DA: Yes, well, in one way, you could say that no one today is as brilliantly intellectual as Chesterton, but you've got a point. Chesterton went through a period of time in his late adolescence/early young adulthood, where he questioned everything, and tried some "dark arts" stuff. He realized he was going down the wrong road after what he believed was a true encounter with the devil himself.

NCB: Speaking of the devil, Potter critics claim that we parents are losing our sense of evil, and that is why we don't recognize how bad the Potter books are for our children. Do you think this is true?

Harry's Enemies Are Really Evil

DA: That's an interesting criticism because one of the things the Harry novels do, I think, is create a story with a real villain, something most modern novelists are unwilling to do.

Harry's enemies are evil. They are not potential converts but fallen angels. They are the enemies that the Psalmist is entitled to "hate with a perfect hatred" while not forgetting to add the prayer, "And see if there be any wicked in me. . ." The main enemy, Voldemort, for starters, murders Harry's parents and tries to murder the infant Harry. He is a baby-

killer and the enemy of everything that is good. He is Satan. Harry's lesser enemies are Draco Malfoy and his father, Lucius Malfoy. Anybody catch any symbolism in those names? Draco's henchmen, Crabbe and Goyle, could easily serve as comical demons in Dante's *Inferno*. But Rowling departs from most modern literature in that there is nothing attractive about her villains. Even their beauty is ugly. Dorothy L. Sayers says that the problem with the Devil on stage is that too often he steals the show. But this doesn't happen in the Potter novels. And Rowling's greatest triumph is that the most fascinating and appealing and completely likeable character is the saintly Dumbledore, who is Harry's chief mentor. He is kind and good and wise. He speaks and acts with authority and draws respect. He has an unwavering sense of justice and mercy. Only those who are openly evil or who are jealous of him, who personify the dictum of the Epistle of St. James, dislike him: "Where jealousy and selfish ambition exist, there will be disorder and every vile practice."

NCB: You said you let your children read Harry Potter, right?

DA: Yes, we've read them and discussed them. And they've re-read them.

Be Suspicious of the Popular Culture

NCB: Okay then, let's talk a little bit about the books' popularity. Some critics seem to think that because the books are popular, we Catholic parents should avoid them like the plague. Why *do* you let your children read them?

DA: First of all, it *is* a good rule of thumb to be suspicious of everything that is popular in our culture, for the simple reason that "popular taste" is usually controlled by very few people with vested interests in determining and controlling those tastes. But every once in a while something is popular because it appeals to the common man. It is popular the way a good song — that is, a song that can be

sung — is popular. There will always be popular literature — not what the public is forced to buy, but what it really wants to read. The mob isn't *always* wrong. In fact, the mob is usually right. Mob rule, says Chesterton, is democracy in its purest form. Not that the mob is always right, but it's generally right more often than the ruling class. The ruling class is never right. Which is why 40 publishers rejected J.K. Rowling's first Harry Potter book before it found its way into print. The snoots who try to control the culture didn't like these books. After all, there is no sex in them, no homosexual heroes, and no suicidal despair.

NCB: I've read several publishers — but not 40 — rejected Sorcerer's (Philosopher's) Stone.

DA: Well, I heard 40, but the point is, it *was* initially rejected. These books go against the stream of modern culture with its relativism and its anti-heroes, and for that matter, its political correctness. That is precisely why parents should be encouraged by Harry Potter. He's an old-fashioned hero. He is moral. He is a boy who is growing in the Christian virtues. He faces hopeless odds and prevails. He believes the incredible and it turns out to be true. He defends the lowly, but he also believes that even giants can be reformed and perhaps even dragons be tamed. He struggles with forgiveness, as do we all. But finds himself forgiven, a creature of Grace. He's like the typical Dickens hero: Pip or David Copperfield. He's humble, he suffers, he endures, and he passes the test. We admire him not because he's a superhero, but because he's brave and loyal. His greatness is achieved in selflessly making the right choices, not only against the odds, but yes, sometimes even against the rules.

NCB: Some critics have characterized the legalism that Harry has to face as a "straw man."

DA: The legalism in the books presents the same obstacle that legalism presents anywhere: laws that are walls without windows, rules that don't recognize exceptions. It is because Harry is good that he doesn't easily break the school

rules. He does so with reluctance, with fear and trembling, and not with a Machiavellian deviousness, as some critics seem to think. He's not a rebel and he isn't proud. He wants what's right but sometimes finds the rules an impediment to what's right, just as the law is sometimes an impediment to justice. The headmaster Dumbledore smiles benevolently on Harry's rule breaking because he knows that Sabbath is made for man not man for the Sabbath.

NCB: What if someone's closed their mind?

Don't Read Harry, Then — Read Chesterton Instead

DA: If someone has closed their mind to the possibility that they might be wrong about Harry Potter, I suppose there is nothing we can do. We can pray for them, I suppose. Although no one *has* to read Harry Potter. The only problem I have with the critics is that they don't allow other parents to use their own brains to decide the answer. And I would recommend that they read Chesterton, as I find him to be the effective guide to all of life's questions, including Harry Potter.

NCB: How has reading Chesterton helped you to think about Harry Potter? And which of Chesterton's works would you recommend to people who don't understand Harry Potter?

DA: "The Ethics of Elfland," from *Orthodoxy*. "The Red Angel" and "The Dragon's Grandmother" from *Tremendous Trifles*, "Magic and Fantasy in Fiction" in *Sidelights*, and *Gilbert Magazine* (see Chesterton Resources at the end of this interview). As I am always trying to point out, Chesterton is a complete thinker. If he is defending fairy tales and stories with magic in them — for which he was criticized in his own day — my money is with Chesterton and not with his critics. I really think the critics of Harry Potter have not thought it out completely.

Not Gnosticism

NCB: Can we talk about another criticism of Harry? Some claim that at their very core, the Potter books are Gnostic. What do you think?

DA: The fact that the wizards segregate themselves from Muggles is a fascinating aspect to the stories, but I don't think we can read Gnosticism into it. There is nothing Gnostic about seeking the Truth, nor in finding it. The Magi could easily be confused with Gnostics. They studied charts nobody else could understand, but the Star they followed led them to Jesus. There is nothing esoteric about Epiphany.

NCB: Chesterton says that every story has a St. George, a dragon and a princess. Obviously, Harry is St. George and Voldemort is the dragon. What or who is the princess?

DA: Hmm. Harry is defending all the good things in life: his friends, his parents' honor, his mentors, his school and its traditions: simply the right order of things which is under attack by chaos and death. But there might be something more to his battles, something more specific that we will discover in the seventh book. When the Seventh Seal is broken!

NCB: Dale, I want to thank you for your Chestertonian perspective on the Harry Potter phenomenon.

DA: You're welcome.

Chesterton Resources

For more information on G.K. Chesterton, the following resources may be a good start:

www.chesterton.org

www.gilbertmagazine.com

The "Red Angel" essay Mr. Ahlquist recommends is in the book *Tremendous Trifles*, which is available online at Project Gutenberg, www.gutenberg.org/etext/8092

"The Dragon's Grandmother" essay is online at

www-personal.umich.edu/~esrabkin/Dragons
   Grandmother.htm

"Magic and Fantasy in Fiction" is available in *Sidelights on New London and Newer York* (London: Sheed and Ward, 1932), p. 230, as well as in Ignatius Press' Collected Works 21.

INTERVIEW WITH REGINA DOMAN

Regina Doman is a children's and young adults' author. She published her first novel for teenagers in 1997: *Snow White and Rose Red: A Modern Fairy Tale* republished in paperback in 2002 under the title *The Shadow of the Bear.* The sequel, *Black as Night*, was published in 2004. Her first picture book, *Angel in the Waters,* has sold 70,000 copies. As an independent contractor she created and is overseeing the development of the *John Paul 2 High series*, novels for teens. Regina is a busy Catholic mother of five, who lives in Virginia.

In many ways, Regina's story mirrors my own: at first, being against the books for what we heard was in them, reading them for ourselves, and coming to enjoy the series. But as a children's book author, Regina brings some unique and interesting ideas into the discussion.

Catholic Moral Framework

Nancy C. Brown (NCB): What do you look for in a good children's book?

Regina Doman (RD): A healthy overlap of the book's moral framework with our own moral framework as Catholic parents. All things being equal, I'd rather my children read books where courage, kindness, honesty, and reverence are honored instead of ignored or laughed at. I'm probably pickier than the average Catholic parent: I get irritated by even hints of anti-religious or anti-Catholic prejudice. And I dislike books that twist history for a politically correct agenda. A book that's grounded in a more

timeless universe is one that I can enjoy and pass on to my children who are still not at the point of choosing their own books — my oldest is 11. *The Tale of Despereaux* is one I recently enjoyed.

NCB: You've read the Potter books, and so have I. But many Catholics haven't, and feel somehow that they shouldn't even read the books if they are filled with evil. What do you say to those parents?

RD: I basically give them my two cents: that the books are not as evil as advertised. But having come full circle in my opinion of the books, I know how much work it took to reverse my opinion, and I can understand if parents don't want to take the trouble I did — namely, reading the entire series twice, the second time reading it with my husband in conjunction with studying John Granger's book *Looking for God in Harry Potter*. As a writer, I have a professional interest in Harry Potter: it's a significant benchmark in children's fiction today and it's in my interest to be "up" on it. A parent who's overwhelmed with other responsibilities and whose children are not particularly drawn to the books might not want to bother about it the way I did.

The Books Generate Discussions

But if I have a sense that the parent in question would benefit from and enjoy the books, I usually encourage them to treat themselves to some good fiction and read the books, maybe with their spouse or their savvy older teenager. The books generate great discussions, and even if you come out disagreeing with Rowling's use of witches and wizards, I don't believe the encounter will harm you.

But I wouldn't condemn someone for refusing to let their children read the books. Humorously, while I sometimes suspect that no one is allowed to enter Heaven until they have finished reading Tolkien's *The Lord of the Rings*, I am still at the point where I believe that one can easily live a full and fruitful Catholic life without entering into the

world of J.K. Rowling. So if parents or teens feel their conscience would not allow them to read the books, I usually tell them not to bother about it.

One exception: anyone planning on writing fiction as a career should read, become familiar with the books, and give them the respect the books are due. Simply because the attitude of *"I, being truly religious, can certainly write better material than that shoddy worldwide bestseller Harry Potter,"* tends to breed an attitude of pride that ruins one's writing and makes one look dim, professionally.

NCB: So, you said you've "come full circle" in your opinion of the books, why were you against the Potter series? What got you to change your mind? How did you discover the series?

Picky, Picky, Picky

RD: I tend to have the snobbish attitude I just mentioned, that most popular literature is absolute rubbish, and I'm overly picky. Please understand that I am serious: my nine siblings hate watching movies with me since I'm the equivalent of the Spanish Inquisition when it comes to examining fiction. I'm not strictly an elitist — I do tend to enjoy popular fiction and there are a few highbrow writers I simply can't enjoy. Unlike J.K. Rowling, I am not a classically trained literature graduate: I majored in television production. But as a writer who has strong opinions, I know the techniques used by writers and directors who have an attitude about their subject or an agenda: I know, because I use those same techniques myself.

So if I believed, for example, that the Vatican is full of power-hungry warlocks, I know how I would incarnate that opinion into a story. This, I guess, makes me better at picking up story cues than other people. So I can't, for example, enjoy a movie like that recent Joan of Arc TV movie starring Leelee Sobieski. To me, it's anti-Catholic. No, not because Peter O'Toole played a great, conflicted bishop

whose conscience and politics force him into burning Joan at the stake. I don't have a problem with that: Peter O'Toole's character is the character I'd use to distract people with. I'd put my hatred of the Catholic Church as a centralized bureaucracy that suppresses truth into a minor character — in this case, the monsignor from Rome who engineers Joan's downfall and maliciously has her raped to break her spirit. That was how I suspect the filmmaker was getting his agenda across — I can't enjoy the movie and I don't know why some Catholic distributors sell it. So, as you can see, I'm pickier than your average Catholic — or above average Catholic — about these things.

So — about Harry Potter, when the books came out, I read a few Catholic reviews and concluded it must be trash. My younger sister, who usually disagrees with me on everything, read the books and characteristically thought they were great. "I don't see anything wrong with them," she said. "My husband and I really enjoyed them." I rattled off the litany of why I thought they were suspect: casting witches as good characters, gross-out humor, Harry lying, being a bad role model, children dabbling in the occult. . . She sort of shrugged, the way she'd shrugged when growing up I had condemned everything from *The Empire Strikes Back* to *Monty Python and the Holy Grail* to *The Princess Bride*. "Yeah, well, I enjoyed it," she said defiantly.

Of course that didn't make any difference to me: in my opinion, my sister had always cut filmmakers and writers way too much slack. But the next time I was over at her house, I picked up her copy of *Harry Potter* and started reading it. I stayed up and finished it that night. The next morning, I blew it off. "It's not any better than Roald Dahl," I told her. And since I dislike Dahl's books, that's hardly a compliment. I read the second book in a similar manner — holding my nose, and was not impressed. However, I did notice that the typical agenda I was used to finding in children's books — humans-are-ruining-the-planet, religion-is-

the-locus-of-all-evil, introduce-kids-to-sex-early, that agenda
— was lacking. And this was a book by *Scholastic*, of all
things, the Mother Lode of Public School Fiction. Usually
children's books, because of their ties to the public school
book market, have an interest in toeing the line politically. I
didn't sense that in the Harry Potter books. I wondered if it
was just because they were British.

The Importance of Fatherhood

But it was when I got to Book Three, which I read with
the encouragement of more like-minded friends, that I
started sitting up and paying attention: Book Three has
fatherhood as a major theme. Not "parenthood," not moth-
erhood — there was no suggestion that Harry should have
been content with his self-sacrificing and heroic mother.
No, Harry acutely longs for his father, and his wish for his
father is fulfilled in a magical way.

Then I started wondering why the "other side" wasn't
boycotting these books.

Children need dads? Since when were we allowed to say
this on the international stage?

I began to get drawn in — I read Books Four and Five
very quickly — within 48 hours of finishing Book Three.
And when I was done I sat on the edge of the bed and
joined the collective howl that Books Six and Seven were
yet to be published. I still thought the books were problematic, but for myself, I was hooked. My husband and I agreed
that we would NOT introduce our children to the books,

More Dinner Table Questions

How is Harry like his father, James? How is he different?
Does Harry want to be like his dad? Do you? How are you
like your parents? How are you different?

but I saw no reason why I shouldn't continue to read them, at least as "research."

But by that time I had grown in respect for Rowling as a writer: maybe I don't recognize good style, but I think Rowling is a fine stylist, at least in that her language enhances and doesn't hinder the storytelling, and she is a master at suspense. I am far from despising the "potboiler, page-turning frenetic style" of the books that some Catholic critics have derided: in my estimation, that's good writing, not bad. Also Rowling's wonderfully strong with characterization: Harry and Hermione are beautifully drawn characters and many of her minor characters are sheer genius: Dickensian. Marvelous plots, good characters and weighty themes — now, why was she supposed to be a poor writer again? My opinion of her changed.

Coming Out of the Closet

In the meantime, I published my second book and was interviewed in a Catholic webzine, and they asked me about Harry Potter. I gave my hesitant approval. Robert Trexler of the C.S. Lewis Society in NYC emailed me then and offered to send me John Granger's book, *Looking for God in Harry Potter*, just to see what I thought of it. I accepted his challenge, and started reading the book. Granger's thesis that Harry Potter is a Christian fiction work was so provocative that I started reading the books again — actually, getting out the excellent audio versions by Jim Dale from our local library and listening to them on tape. My husband began listening too, and reading John Granger's book alongside me. We were forced to revise our opinions by John's excellent arguments and explanations of the difference between incantational and invocational magic. I'm really very indebted to him for my "conversion."

NCB: What do you do in your home to help your children deal with the witchcraft, the themes of evil and death, and the spells, potions, and charms?

RD: I think that my children have been able to intuit the differences themselves. They can *tell* it's a different magic than the kind forbidden by the First Commandment. And this might point out the difficulty with Harry Potter: I think lots of people can intuit that the books feel "safe" but they can't explain why. But other people, maybe more rational types, are thrown by the language of "witch," "wizard," etc. And all their alarm bells go off, and they can't understand why other people don't see the problems they see.

The Biggest Problem with Harry Potter

The biggest problem with Harry Potter that I see is the mutual frustration it unwittingly generates between very good people, one side thinking that it's obvious that there's nothing wrong with the books, the other side thinking it's obvious that there is a good deal wrong with them. Harry Potter has been the cause of unkindness on both sides — both sides calling each other blind and stupid and obstinate and endangering everything from the Faith itself to the status of devout Catholics as intelligent human beings.

My children are basically unaware of the controversy: however, we have told them that some of our friends aren't comfortable with Harry Potter and don't want their children reading it. So we have let our children know that Harry Potter is something that we just enjoy as a family ourselves. We have, on the other hand, absolutely forbidden our children from sneering at those who don't like or fear the books.

I constantly quiz our children about fiction, and in a few instances where I disagree with Harry's actions or think they might be misleading, I'll say things like, "Should Harry have done that? Wouldn't it have have been better for him to ask a grownup for help?" My children give the right answers, and I feel comfortable that they're getting the right message.

I don't feel the themes of death and evil are overwhelmingly too hard for them: generally I like how Rowling approaches the

subject. But my husband did feel the fourth movie was too intense for them to see in the theaters so we waited for the DVD. But our children are young. Plus we don't own the books so it is easier to regulate their use in our family.

NCB: Have you read the books aloud? Did/do you read them with your children? At what age, in your opinion, could a child read Harry by himself — and this may be different ages for different titles?

Don't Rush Harry

RD: I don't know when I'd let my children read them on their own — age 14, maybe, for my son. The books are such a treat and get better with re-reads, that I'd encourage families to listen to them together with their children. Definitely different ages for different children. There are some things that shouldn't be rushed, and Harry is one of them. I could see the books being a good present for a young teenager.

NCB: As a writer of fiction for young people, what do you see in the Potter books that is good, and fulfills the requirements of a good story? Is there anything bad? Or things you don't/didn't like? How is it as literature?

RD: As I said, I came to respect Rowling as a writer, and she has many qualities I find particularly attractive: good characters, humor, suspense, and weighty themes. As I read them, I began to sense that the books had a moral consistency that was in some ways out of step with what passes for mainstream morality. Certainly Rowling talks a lot about tolerance for differences, that perennial lesson hammered home on so many hapless schoolchildren — what did schoolchildren *read* about in the benighted past when tolerance wasn't the paragon of all virtues, I wonder? And she also talks about loyalty towards one's friends, etc.

But she doesn't rant about saving the planet, and she doesn't — despite many openings for her to do it — make snide remarks about folks in the past hating witches

because of ignorance and superstition. This is a glaring omission. As the books go on, Rowling speaks less and less about Muggle's hatred of magic and more and more about the responsibility magical folk have to be kind and forbearing with Muggles. If Rowling wanted to score points against Christian fundamentalists, she could easily work some cheap shots into the rich tapestry of human foibles she's created. But there's nothing of the sort in the books — no Roman inquisitors haunting the shadows, no lectures about oppression and the opium of the people. Many of Rowling's fans sneer at religion, but she never does. Why not? I suspect it is because she is charitable — a huge deal, and because she actually has reverence towards religion.

Revolutionary Words

In addition, the way she can verbalize a moral truth in a nutshell is brilliant: for example, Dumbledore's observation in Book Four that at some point, everyone must make a choice "between what is right and what is easy." Since most public schools aren't allowed to teach that there is such a thing as right and wrong, such words are almost revolutionary.

And the sexual restraint of the best characters, such as Hermione, is remarkable, together with the relative sexual innocence of the rest of the lot. It is amazing that there are no divorced wizards, or wizards "living together" or otherwise involved in sexual sins that are taken for granted today. True, in Book Six, there was a lot of "snogging," what Americans term "making out," but it's interesting that there's not a single reference, even obliquely, to safe sex.

I explained how picky I am: these books did not trip my alarm bells at all regarding religion, the Church, Christianity. And that is amazing.

Whatever her own personal religious convictions, Rowling's stories have a strong moral anchor in Dumbledore and Hermione, and Harry himself grows stronger in virtue

as the series goes on. As he grows in power, he learns, "with great power, comes great responsibility." And even more than being merely moral, the stories make goodness fun — attractive and beautiful and something to long for. The goodness in the Weasley family, in the friendship and cama-raderie of the Gryffindor, of the adventure and excitement of Quidditch — all the good things about the world of Rowling are so much more alluring than the grim masks and cold pride of the Death Eaters. Most fantasy writers aside from Lewis and Tolkien skimp on the "good side" and adorn their evil characters with interest and glamour. Rowling doesn't. Lord Voldemort isn't half as interesting as Dumbledore. Bellatrix Lestrange isn't as fascinating as Sir-ius Black, Harry's godfather. And, like Tolkien, Rowling excels in a variety of her good characters: Lupin, Mad Eye Moody, Dumbledore, Luna, Mrs. Weasley, Tonks — all of them are so *different* in the way they choose to fight for the good, while all Death Eaters are pretty much alike. That is a phenomenal achievement in a day and age where only the black hats have any real dramatic interest and the white hats are dull and limp.

I don't like that Rowling seems to have a cavalier atti-tude to "white lies" or lies told in the line of duty. I don't believe in telling white lies, and the few times where Hermione, the moral anchor, lies needlessly really irk me. I am willing to excuse it, especially when Harry suffers so many times for telling the truth when it's not popular.

NCB: You believe that Rowling's work is "Christian fic-tion in disguise", as you said in your article. What makes a work of fiction "Christian"?

RD: Oh dear, not that controversy. Lest the term "Chris-tian fiction" be generalized into non-existence, I will define why I think that Harry Potter specifically is Christian: I am trusting John Granger's hunch that the books are actually an allegory of the Christian soul being purified by Christ, and that all of the various emblems and symbols that Rowl-

ing uses — everything from the Golden Lion of Gryffindor House to Fawkes the Phoenix to the Philosopher's Stone — Book 1 to the Stag Patronus that saves Harry in Book Three to the negative evidence that Rowling's evil manifests itself as "Death Eaters" — Christians are "Life Eaters" — whose followers kill unicorns, Christ symbols, and perform an "un-baptism" in Book Four, and split their souls to escape death in Book Six — everything is servicing that allegory.

So when I say that Harry Potter is Christian fiction in disguise, I'm throwing in my lot with the Eastern Orthodox homeschool dad, John Granger. I don't mean that the books are morally Christian or Catholic in some vague universal sense, or that they affirm my personal understanding of Catholicism or Christianity — I mean that I suspect they are a deliberate attempt by a Christian author to pen an elaborate, painstaking, and very well-thought-out Christian allegory, an allegory that is now so ancient and ridiculed and forgotten that most people can't even recognize it for what it is.

Rowling may never be forthcoming with her intention — if I were her, I wouldn't — so we may never know for sure. If I were she, I would trust that part of the power of the Christian allegory is that it is hidden, almost subliminal. Explaining it would rob it of its power to draw the unbeliever in with his guard lowered.

NCB: Do Rowling's personal beliefs play into this at all? If she's Christian, does that make it a Christian book? What if she really isn't Christian? Does it matter what kind of person she is?

RD: Oh, if she turns out to be a Buddhist, then we can certainly credit her with being completely dysfunctional in her personal beliefs and her writing. Her imagination seems to be thoroughly Christian and how rare that is. From my point of view, it certainly matters what her beliefs are, but I'm very, very picky, as I explained before.

If she isn't a Christian, then the book isn't "Christian" by the standards I outlined above, but I'm sure it's Christian in

the more vague, metaphorical sense — the sense in which *Fiddler on the Roof* could be called "Christian." It occupies the Christian moral universe, intentionally or not. Either way, the books are quite an achievement.

NCB: I know you are a Chestertonian. Does Chesterton have anything to say that helped you in thinking about Harry Potter? Would Chesterton have liked Harry Potter, do you think?

RD: Oh, I'm sure he would have. He would have had fun explaining that the stories aren't merely moral, so of course they seem pagan. He could come up with the other half of the paradox too, I'm sure.

NCB: Has Harry Potter helped your family in any way?

RD: It's definitely made ten-hour-car-trips through Indiana and Michigan so much more bearable. The stories are great to read, listen to, and re-read.

NCB: Thank you, Regina, for your insights into the fiction of J.K. Rowling.

RD: You're welcome.

Regina Doman's website is www.reginadoman.com.

Dale and Regina have shared some great thoughts with us about Rowling. One of the strongest things to note is that they both read the Harry Potter books to their children. There is value in reading all kinds of books together. Even books one considers "bad," when read together, can be a source of learning, conversation, and character-building. I do not believe the Harry Potter books are such "bad" books. However, I've read about families reading books together such as Pullman's *His Dark Materials*, which are overtly anti-God and anti-church. These families read this book because it's popular, and they help their children discern what is wrong with the book. Teens learn so much more by going through books with their parents than they would if left on their own.

Appendix B

For Teachers and Catechists
(and Parents, Too)

For those who teach Catholic students, the Harry Potter books can be a great source of discussion materials. The only problem here is that some parents might not want their children reading Harry Potter. Please consider this as you talk to your students about the Potter series. You may want to recommend *The Mystery of Harry Potter* to those parents who are undecided about Rowling's books. I commend you for doing so.

For those students who have read Harry Potter, you can often find good examples of situations in the books to explain a point of religion or faith. The ability to do so, however, implies that *you've* read the books.

Rowling has created a whole world, an entire set of people, places, and things. If you don't know who Dumbledore, Voldemort, and Mad Eye are; if you haven't heard of a Tri-Wizard Tournament, the Ministry of Magic lackey Professor Umbridge, or a horcrux; if you can't understand what Dumbledore's Army or Fred and George's Joke Shop is, you need to read Harry Potter. You will have to do this so you can speak the language; so you can understand the plots; so you can make the connections for your students. I highly recommend you begin reading the Potter books now, and you will be writing to thank me once you enter the Potter world.

For those who *have* read the Potter books, I feel certain that you are bright enough to see many, many ways in which you can use the material to begin discussions in your

classroom. However, in the spirit of helpfulness, I'll give some ideas for discussion starters here.

I recommend confining your discussions to the books, not the movies, unless your students are much older. The books contain much more "meat" for classroom discussion.

Suggested Questions for Discussion

Basic Harry Potter Questions

1. Ask your students which of the characters they think they are most like, and why?
2. What character do they dislike and why?
3. Which character do they think is the smartest? Most helpful? Least helpful?
4. How is their school like Hogwarts? How is Hogwarts different?
5. Which of the Harry Potter students do they wish was in their class? Why?

Harry Potter Stuff/Materialism

1. Do you have to buy stuff to enjoy Harry Potter?
2. How do companies try to get children to buy Harry Potter games, action figures, and other collectibles? Are they taking unfair advantage of the fact that children like Harry Potter?
3. How can we fight against materialism in regard to Harry Potter?
4. Is materialism wrong? Why?

The Bible and the Catechism

Spend some time and look up the Bible and *Catechism* references to witchcraft and the occult. Teach your children that we don't believe in calling on spirits or mixing potions to trick people into doing or saying things they don't want to do or say. You can tell your students that J.K. Rowling,

the author of Harry Potter, does not believe that witchcraft is okay, or that children will get interested in the occult from reading her books. We all agree that it's wrong.

1. Why are tarot card reading, palm reading, crystal ball gazing, and anything like that wrong?

2. If people can see the future, isn't that a gift? There was a girl in the New Testament who could see the future. What happened to her? (See Acts 16:16.)

3. Why would making potions be wrong? What if you could have a happiness potion? Wouldn't that be good?

4. What kind of power does God give us if we follow him closely? Is it anything like magic?

Morality

1. What are morals? Are they the same as values? Are they the same as virtues?

2. What kind of morals do you follow? What are the rules of your home? Of your school? Are rules good? Why?

3. What kind of morals does the world have? What are the rules of our world? Are the rules good? Are they always good? Why or why not?

4. What virtues should you try to gain? Which ones are important? Why?

Magic

1. Is magic bad? Have you ever seen a magic show? What kind of magic is good? What kind might be bad? Do we have to be careful with magic?

2. What is "black magic" and what does that mean?

3. Are magicians bad? Are they good? Are they good or bad because they do magic?

4. Are magic words okay to use? What do they mean?

Defense Against the Dark Arts

1. How could you apply Defense Against the Dark Arts lessons with Harry to your own life today? What do you need to defend yourself against?
2. Are there any problems in your life that you need to practice working on ways to fix? Do you ever have temptations to do things you shouldn't?
3. What are some ways the Church gives us to defend ourselves against the "dark"?

Is Harry Just Lucky?

1. Is Harry really just a lucky kid? What's lucky about him? What isn't so lucky?
2. In what ways is your life lucky or we might call it blessed?
3. In what ways is your life hard? Is your life as hard as Harry's? Why or why not?
4. Does Harry have a lot of friends in school? How come some kids don't like him? Is Harry popular? Why or why not?

Does Harry Get Adults to Solve His Problems?

1. When Harry has a problem, whom does he go to for help?
2. Should adults help Harry? Or should Harry solve his own problems?
3. How do you know when you can do something yourself, and when you need an adult's help?
4. Who are the safe adults in your life who can help you when you need help?

Friendships

1. Who are Harry's closest friends who are his age? Who are his closest adult friends?

2. What does Harry do that makes him a good friend? What does Harry do that isn't so good for friendships?
3. How does Harry make new friends? Do you have trouble making new friends?
4. Some people say that to have a friend, "be a friend." What kinds of things should you do to "be a friend"?

Heroes

1. Who are some of your favorite heroes?
2. Is Harry Potter a hero? Why or why not?
3. What do heroes do? How do heroes act?
4. Could you be heroic? Why or why not?

Love

1. What is love? How do you show love? What does the world say love is? What does God say about love?
2. Is there anything you love so much you'd be willing to die for it? Would you die for God, like the martyrs did? Would you die for your parents? A sibling? Would you die for your country?
3. Does fighting for something mean you love it? Could you fight for a bad cause? How do loving something and fighting for it go together? Is fighting always wrong?
4. How can the examples of love in Harry Potter help us love our families and friends more?

Christian Symbolism

1. What are symbols and where do you usually find them? Have you ever seen anything in church that is symbolic? Why do people use symbols to represent Christian ideas?
2. If you find Christian symbols in a book or in a piece of art, does that mean that the thing is Christian? Could it be a coincidence?

3. What examples of Christian symbolism can you find in Harry Potter? What did you think about when you found that? Do Christian symbols help us to think about God?

4. Find an art book and look up the "code" of Christian symbols. You might find a peacock, or a pelican, or an anchor. Can you think of a symbol for something important to your faith? What is it? What does it stand for?

Recommended Books to Have at Home for Harry Potter Discussions

A Catholic Bible, such as *The Ignatius Bible: Revised Standard Version* (RSV)
The Catechism of the Catholic Church

Bibliography

Websites

www.harrypotter.com
www.the-leaky-cauldron.org
www.jkrowling.com
www.mugglematters.com
www.hogwartsprofessor.com
www.hp-lexicon.org
www.chesterton.org

Book Review Websites

www.love2learn.net
www.whippersnapperbooks.com
www.amazon.com   (I use this site for secular books, reading a large number of reviews while checking who wrote the review, what they believe, etc.)

Parent Resources

www.christianbookguides.com   (For a free download-able discussion guide for parents based on the John Granger book *Looking for God in Harry Potter*.)

Books

Anatol, Giselle Liza (Ed.). *Reading Harry Potter: Critical Essays*. Westport, CT: Praeger Publishers, 2003.

Bridger, Francis. *A Charmed Life: The Spirituality of Potterworld*. New York: Image Books (Doubleday), 2002.

Chesterton, G.K. *Lepanto, with Explanatory Notes and Commentary*, edited by Dale Ahlquist. Minneapolis, MN: American Chesterton Society, 2003. [Permission to use Commentary and Notes granted by Dale Ahlquist.]

Chesterton, G.K. *Tremendous Trifles*. New York: Sheed & Ward, 1909.

Chesterton, G.K. *The Everlasting Man*. Collected Works, Volume 2, p. 317. Ignatius Press, 1986.

Chesterton, G.K. *Orthodoxy*. Collected Works, Volume 1, p. 303. Ignatius Press, 1987.

Fleming, Thomas. *The Morality of Everyday Life: Rediscovering an Ancient Alternative to the Liberal Tradition*. Columbia and London: University of Missouri Press, 2004.

Granger, John. *Looking for God in Harry Potter*. SaltRiver (Tyndale imprint), 2004.

Harry Potter and Philosophy: If Aristotle Ran Hogwarts, ed. Baggett, David, and Shawn E. Klein. Chicago: Open Court, 2004.

Kern, Edmund. *The Wisdom of Harry Potter: What Our Favorite Hero Teaches Us about Moral Choices*. Amherst, NY: Prometheus Books, 2003.

Nel, Philip. *J.K. Rowling's Harry Potter Novels: A Reader's Guide*. New York: Continuum, 2001.

Rowling, J.K. *Harry Potter and the Sorcerer's Stone*. New York: Arthur A. Levine Books (Scholastic), 1997.

Rowling, J.K. *Harry Potter and the Chamber of Secrets*. New York: Arthur A. Levine Books (Scholastic),1999.

Rowling, J.K. *Harry Potter and the Prisoner of Azkaban*. New York: Arthur A. Levine Books (Scholastic), 1999.

Rowling, J.K. *Harry Potter and the Goblet of Fire*. New York: Arthur A. Levine Books (Scholastic), 2000.

Rowling, J.K. *Harry Potter and the Order of the Phoenix*. New York: Arthur A. Levine Books (Scholastic), 2003.

Rowling, J.K. *Harry Potter and the Half-Blood Prince*. New York: Arthur A. Levine Books (Scholastic), 2005.

Rowling, J.K. *Harry Potter and the Deathly Hallows*. New York: Arthur A. Levine Books (Scholastic), 2007.

Magazine Articles

Ahlquist, Dale. "Sometimes You Have to Fight: A Chestertonian Perspective." *Catholic Men's Quarterly* (Summer/Fall 2006): 5-6.

Birmingham, Carrie. "Harry Potter and the Baptism of the Imagination." *Stone-Campbell Journal* (Issue 8 , Vol. 2): 199-214.

Caldecott, Leonie. "Surprised by Joy: Children's Literature and the Search for Meaning." *The Chesterton Review* (Vol. 31, No. 3&4, Fall/Winter 2005). South Orange, NJ: Seton Hall University, pp.125-139.

Dailey, Sean P. "At Play in Potter's Field." *Gilbert Magazine* (July/August 2001).

Deavel, Catherine Jack and David Paul Deavel. "Character, Choice and Harry Potter." *Logos* (5:4, Fall 2002): 49-64.

Jacobs, Alan. "Harry Potter's Magic." *First Things* (Jan. 2000): 35-38.

Please see www.mrsnancybrown.blogspot.com for additional books, magazine articles, and on-line articles about Harry Potter.

For more information from Nancy Carpentier Brown on Harry Potter, go to

www.osv.com/harrypotter

Including:

Reflections on the seventh Harry Potter book, *Harry Potter and the Deathly Hallows*

An expanded bibliography of materials about the Harry Potter books